THE TRICKY TEENS

Handle with love & care

Bhavna Karnani Killa

First published in 2021 by

BecomeShakespeare.com

One Point Six Technologies Pvt. Ltd.
119-123, 1st floor, Building No. J2, Wadala East,
Wadala Truck Terminal, Mumbai, Maharashtra 400037, India
T: +91 8080226699

ISBN: 978-93-5458-584-5

DEDICATED

With love and luck to the teenagers especially to my kids; also,
to you, the lovely readers.

ACKNOWLEDGEMENTS

The Tricky Teens is a book based on teen tantrums, fights, moments of love, tears, appreciation, criticism, and my lectures, with some research done about teenagers' minds. I have preserved my experiences to publish them for you. When I began writing this book, I did not know that my girls would grow quicker than this book. By the time this is printed, they will be old enough to understand the chapters with more maturity than today. I might not have been a gentle critique, and they might have had opposing thoughts. But when they find this book on the upper shelf sometime later in life, I'm sure they will dust it to find stories quite relatable and matching ideas in those years. They will have more stories to add. I might then not be there for offering any opinion, so I herewith thankfully toast "Cheers! to my motherhood and their teenage years!"

I extend my heartfelt gratitude to all those who have been a part of my journey. Especially my husband Gaurav for his unshakable support in every way and his trust in me always. The fact that you are always there for me is one of the many amazing things about you, and that I count myself lucky to have you. I am grateful to my children Tanvi and Avni for giving me the motherhood experience and being my inspiration forever. Thank you for giving me fair inputs and sharing your thoughts about various topics. Without feedback from both of you, this book would not be possible for sure. Thank you for being my co-authors!

I respectfully extend my gratitude to Mumma and Papa for giving me the upbringing I received. I am fortunate to be raised by my parents for all the precious values I inherited. I am happy to become the individual I am today. Special thanks to my father for his precious time and for helping me edit this book, without which it would not be so fluent. Thank you, papa! You have always been my writing guide.

I thank my sister, who has always heard me and guided me through this journey. I am thankful to my family and friends who have always backed me in bringing out my passion for writing and have shared their experiences as parents. To my friends on social media for their appreciation, comments, likes, and much love! To all my life's critics whose opinions help me become better, strengthen my will to write, and help me grow.

I thank all my teachers for giving me the knowledge to express myself in words. I thank the teachers and counselors of my kids who have given me the vision to understand my children from a different perspective altogether! Special mention of Meetu Chawla for being a dear friend and the best counselor. Thankyou for being there as a coach and mentor to guide and help my children.

I thank the editing and publishing team of BecomeShakespeare.com for publishing my book. Thankful for your guidance and for turning my manuscript into a book.

Special thanks to my daughter Tanvi for putting forward her ideas in designing the book cover. Thank you so much baby.

I thank all the mothers and children who shared their stories; and all my readers who found this book worthy of reading.

I thank my house help and all the other staff members who have helped me finish the daily chores and thus provided me time to write.

I am thankful to my late grandmother, who has played an incredible role in my childhood. I thank her for scolding me, for the life lessons she gave me through the mythological stories. Even though I was not fortunate enough to have her for many years, I am thankful to her for being an integral part of my upbringing.

I am thankful to my late father-in-law for always watching over me and showering his blessings from above.

I am thankful to God, the supernatural powers, my guiding angels, my guiding lights, healing angels, the divine souls, and Master; for their blessings, guidance, support, and strength. Thank you all!

ABOUT THE BOOK

The relationship between a parent and child is exciting and tricky, especially when they are tweens or teens. 'The Tricky Teens' is an effort to show ways to make the 'tricky' part 'easy' through factual incidents and stories. It is like any other story that we can read from more than one side. A one-sided story is like watching a movie on a half-covered screen. This book attempts to show both sides, the entire screen. This ability to see both perspectives of the same situation is an essential life skill for each of us today. To know other people's outlook and understanding the situation from their point of view, simultaneously our ability to introspect our feelings and actions about the circumstance will help solve most of the issues.

Despite all the love and care, we do have moments when we fail to consider the other person, be it a child or a parent, as an individual. We see the other only as per the part they play in our lives.

The Tricky Teens has chronicled some authentic incidents that encase some fun facts, which will entertain and shall also prove to be learning lessons. These profound learnings are very much relatable to the parent-teen duo of prevailing time and age. This book is an effort to help us not judge others by their roles but to appreciate them as individual souls. For this, we need to barter feelings by breaking the barrier in our bias minds.

Mother and daughter share one of the cutest relationships in the world. This book explores the day-to-day cute, naughty, sweet, and sour relationship between them. The readers can relate to the generalised ideas in this book. It has got nothing to do with anyone's life specifically and surely nothing to offend anyone. And yes, because I have two daughters, I have referred to all the examples with context to daughters, so *do not think that the book isn't for sons*!

The ideas in this book can be liberating for both parents and teens as they can help relate to the phase they are going through. This book can even help communicate their feelings to one another about whatsoever is going on in their mind while reading it. The Tricky Teens shall help parents and teens to overcome their hitches about doing things or doing things in a certain way together. When there is open communication, life can be livelier and refreshing while hesitations and fears fade away. I am sure you will find multiple ideas in the book to make this transition easy for both your kids and you.

We want our kids to be rooted and have wings to fly high at the same time. There comes a time when we realise that the roots seem to be disappearing while their wings grow and flutter, restless to fly. It is then time for us to know that we have entered a new world of parenting, that we are now parents of teenagers!

These little ones and not so little ones begin to develop a mind of their own and want to rule their world with their approach. It is the stage where most parents and kids come into conflicts with one another. Well! It is a scary proposition for us as parents because we wish them to remain our 'babies' forever and simultaneously want them to grow up and be responsible.

So let us, as parents, understand that we imprudently wish our kiddies to not only remain under our guidance but also want them to be responsible and make their own decisions. Yet, again we even choose for them where they can make their own decisions. We treat them like kids but expect them to behave like adults and ultimately confuse these innocently growing souls.

As for the parents, upbringing their teens is a full-time challenge. Similarly, it is a painful job for teens to figure out this transitional stage from childhood to 'challenge hood' or pre-adolescence. These half-baked muffins are mostly on trial to figure out their parents' mindset; parents with constant pressure and heat of expectations foresee them become fluffy cakes. While trying to understand and perceive the world beyond their comfort zone, these grown-up babies have different experiences. Amidst parental naggings and peer pressure, they find life to be challenging, beautiful, hilarious, heart-warming, and sometimes disappointing too. These life's happy and sad incidents become lessons for both parents and teens. You will find one such incident in almost all chapters trying to tell the story from both sides, showing the entire screen. These essential lessons shall help both the parties to understand each other better, forge stronger ties and develop affectionate bonds. I am sure you will find multiple ideas in the book to make this transition easy for both parents and kids. I must add a word of caution. These ideas herein are not set in stone, and you can adapt them as per your circumstances.

In this world of Teenagers, emotions flow, sentiments rise, arguments take place both sweet and bitter, parents are mostly bewildered, and teens perplexed. This bracket of age has always been different from all other stages of life.

The Tricky Teens brings out a glimpse of what goes on in the minds of teenagers and their parents. It is a difficult period for the parents as much as it is for the teenagers themselves. Let us together experience the daily flow of emotions, tantrums, drama, and much love!

-Bhavna Karnani Killa
Author: "Bee Magical"
Email: trickyteensbybhavna@gmail.com

ABOUT THE AUTHOR

Bhavna was born and brought up in the City of Joy, Kolkata. She is a mother of two beautiful teenage daughters studying in La Martiniere for Girls School. Bhavna is an ardent writer working as a content creator. She inherited the passion of writing from her father and has been writing articles for magazines and newspapers. She is the author of a self-help book Bee Magical which has been blessed with many awards, and was published in October 2019.

She has also made a mark in child psychology, qualified from IGNOU. Also taken montessori training from Calcutta Montessori Training Centre and served as a Montessori Teacher. Bhavna is the former CEO of the activity centre named Bee's Academy.

She is designated as the National Vice President at WICCI (Women's Indian Chamber of Commerce and Industry), National Child Care Council. Bhavna is also a pranic healer and has been a motivational speaker at Divine Spark Pranic Healing Centre.

She as a home maker steals quality time for her family and herself from daily chores. The idea of writing this book got conceptualised in her me-time sessions during the lockdown period. She has been thoroughly supported by her husband for all her endeavours which finally makes her feel proud of all her achievements till date.

Connect with her at trickyteensbybhavna@gmail.com

CONTENTS

CHAPTER -1

HEY...WHAT'S UP?

Hey there...! The young reader of my book, I welcome you to The Tricky Teens. Parents! you are welcome too!

We all know that "teens" begin their journey from thirteen and end at nineteen years of age. But even if you are 12 years, or 20 years old or more, it does not matter. I am open to friendship with any age group, and so is this book...what about you? Let us be friends and explore this adventurous journey together. Moreover, this adventure will be incomplete without the parents

Well, let me introduce myself first. I am Bhavna, and I have written this book to understand you 'the teens' better. I also aim to help other parents to understand and get closer to their teens. I am glad that it reached you, and all you need to do is read it! I suggest, read it with a pencil and scribble down your thoughts as they arise. Also, mark the portion that you identify with so closely.

It feels so good to know that quite a few teens still read these days. Reading certainly does not mean that you go for storybooks or novels only. Read the stuff of your choice or whatsoever you can lay your hands upon; it is more important to engage yourself in reading. It is fun, I'm telling you! It is said, *"Reading is to the mind what exercise is to the body."* You may Google to find out more about the benefits of reading. Also, of course, indulging in reading does not mean flipping through the books the entire day. It depends on your interest, on how long you would want to engage yourself with words.

To tell you a little more about me, my first book 'Bee Magical' deals with easy techniques of creating life in the way you want it to be.

13

It helps to discover the incredible power that lies within all of us. Well, there I have taken the example of the honey bees as they are hard-working and well-organised social creatures. They bring forth inspiration and magically turn their life beautiful, thus the name "Bee Magical." I believe you will enjoy it.

Okay, now back to this book. I have written this book for you and me to understand each other and help create a cohesive unit of teens and their parents. My inspiration is my two daughters, who are almost 15 and 12 years old respectively, and of course you, the teen-kids. They will almost turn 16 and 13 by the time this manuscript turns into a book.

I clearly understand that the 'TEEN LIFE' is thoroughly different; they have a Universe of their own. There are too many things to handle simultaneously, and I understand that it becomes nerve-racking for you guys with all the stress and anxiety. Emotional damages in the form of agony, misery, and suffering certainly happen due to some repeated course of action or pressure. Even if you are a recently retired teenager, you know how it feels to be one, and you will be able to relate to these facts about the Teen world.

To begin from parents' point of view, let us talk about health issues which is commonly an irritating topic for children. Oh! I'm sorry if it is too annoying to talk about giving up on unhealthy food like your fav' junkies- pizza, nachos, or Aglio olio; and taking up a healthy food regime. Anyways, let me touch on the topic in short! That may be a favourite one for parents.

Do you feel the need to bring down your weight, reduce in inches, build muscles, get taller, become fairer, or get rid of that stubborn acne? It is then you finally think of trying out a new lifestyle altogether. You feel like making a diet and exercise plan and want to follow it, but you give up due to lack of discipline. You resolve to take action to make life better; unfortunately, your taste buds seem to disturb you, and you get influenced by the 'buddy code.' Mind says, "How can I upset my friends by not joining them for lunch or any other outing?" That usually happened to me. Do you face similar situations too?

Enough of food-talk, right? Let us switch to a fascinating conversation like Friends...best friends...boyfriends, BFFs!? Do you like or dislike anyone for so many odd reasons...? To be more specific, are you having a crush or dating or roasting someone? Well, if I'm not wrong most of you refer to ragging as roasting; to be clear, it is an act of humiliating or criticising.

For many 'tweens' and young teenagers, the word dating amounts to socialising one to one. Having a boyfriend/ girlfriend has become more of a social symbol in your Teen World, rather than understanding the actual meaning of 'to be in a relationship.' That is one reason we use terms like 'puppy love' and 'crush' to describe teenage romances or infatuations. At times, you need to boast that indeed you have a girl/boyfriend too since other friends of your group already have. You desperately require a girl/boyfriend so that you can be an active part of the conversation when your friends talk about theirs. More so, you have someone to make online conversations with and spend almost the entire day chatting about each other's likes and dislikes.

There are endless things we can discuss about this tricky age. Apart from the good side, we also have a frightful side of this phase in life. Taking up cheap and unwanted dares from friends while playing the most indulging game of your generation- 'truth and dare' becomes very thrilling.

Some of your so-called 'normal' experiences include trying alcohol, puffing on a cigarette, enjoying 'Shisha' (commonly known as hookah), rash driving, illegally riding bikes, and performing daring stunts. Intake of drugs just for the heck of it has also become a part among the teens. Some of you might have come out of all this or maybe, going through similar experiences right now. How do you feel about them?

Some of you may have enjoyed them thoroughly. Post your teenage, some of you might have got into a serious job to make your career bright and beautiful. While some of you must have initially enjoyed these above-mentioned teenage experiences; and have repented later in the form of ill health, low performance, emotional issues, mood fluctuations, depression, and many more. Some of you might even as well regret that time has flown never to return as you have already lost a good deal of it. So everyone has a different approach towards life and has different perceptions about similar things.

Well, children, do your parents and guardians keep nagging as if they have no other work in their life? Are they always ready with their patent dialogues about being organised? About screen time... junk food...dressing style...studies...sleeping pattern...outings...phone calls...? OMG, I swear it is too much for you to handle!

If only you could keep your parents away from poking their nose into your matters, you might be able to live life a little stress-free. Schoolwork, be it incomplete classwork, homework, notes, projects, and grades, these are your everyday concerns. No amount of work can ever satisfy parents' expectations, and it keeps burdening you more.

Times have changed; what used to be a playground in the park earlier is in cyberspace now. Family time has shortened, and there is hardly any 'me-time.' Your schedule gets divided into friends-time, or the gadget-time, screen time, and of course, you need them all. Apart from cyberspace, you require outdoor playtime, sleeping time, even television time, etc.

You have too much to do and very little time to finish them all. It is frustrating when time and task remain unmatched due to many reasons. On top of it, you constantly get reminded by your parents of your performance. You do not feel good about yourself. You would want to crawl inside a hole with your phone and talk about it with a friend who 'understands.'

I agree it feels better when you have 'bitched' about your situation to your friends and is a sure-shot way of releasing stress. During our days also teenage used to be a roller coaster ride, so is yours now; but the situations are purely different. Ah! Parents have a bad habit of mentioning "our times" whenever they begin a conversation, I know, right? They need to get rid of this!

Few thoughts or questions might quite frequently arise about your own identity. You wonder who you are and the purpose of your life; you even get confused about your career. You certainly develop a perception about yourself based on other's opinions about you and wonder how the other people appraise (judge) you? You may become indecisive about your future, doubting your capabilities.

Nonstop nagging, restrictions, poking noses, regular complaining, big expectations, getting hyper...all that I have just mentioned is what the parents do! Ooh! It is too much for you to handle, of course. But then these problems as you perceive them are real, and you need to face them all. There is no delete button to erase them, so don't even expect to get away from them smoothly, rather deal with them smartly. All these are parent's genuine efforts to be concerned and care for your wellness.

"Either parent get hyper for little things, or they don't care at all!" That is a typical remark of teens today. Here, I would like to ask all the teenagers - *Despite your parents' love and care, is that what you think of your parents when they try to guide you, discipline you, make you stronger and get you ready to face the real world?*

It might sound strange to some of you, yet you have to believe that - every parent wants the best for their child. They might have a different opinion than yours for a similar kind of situation. You may feel what is good about putting restrictions on every damn thing. Well, there has to be some logic in it. I agree, else it is wrong to restrict. Then again, the logic is theirs and usually differs from yours. Mostly their logic is your wellbeing.

I need to tell you although you might already know. Teenage is a golden period in one's life; the adults reminisce about it. It is also an age where all kids wish to reach quickly. And why not...? it is good to be a grown-up and yet not that old ☺.

Well, teenage or adolescence is a time of rapid growth, rapid change in you. The 'change' is all-around, and you have to deal with it physically, emotionally, and socially. I understand these changes do create stress and put you in an abnormal state of worry. One important thing that you must learn during your teenage is to shield yourself with facts and carry confidence as your self-defence tools. This armour will help you fight all anxiety and will surely safeguard you from the uncertainty that otherwise might shroud you.

In this book, I have tried to figure out solutions to these 'real' problems. We know that we cannot just erase. Problems can be many and are different for individuals. Before moving on to the solutions, let us understand that the situations you have in your life are different from the ones your friend faces. Every family has its own unique set of principles which includes liberty as well as restrictions. So, solutions are exclusive too.

NOTE FOR PARENTS: Girls and boys of standard sixth feel enthused to have a boyfriend or a girlfriend. Girls begin 'dating' maybe as early as eleven or twelve, and boys a year older. But it may not be the dating that you are picturing as a parent.

There has always been a fantasy world away from the actual, where teens live, and it still exists for teens of today. They have their world of expectations and socialising altogether.

Disclaimer: As mentioned earlier, this book speaks a lot about my experiences, and I have written in context to daughters. But yes, more content has been added. It has nothing to do with anyone's personal life. Be rest assured that the book is not gendered biased and recommended for all.

CHAPTER 2

THE SEA-SAW OF TROUBLE-HOOD

Parents of today are certainly different than a generation back when they were themselves, kids. They have seen a more rapid change in their childhood compared to yours, and the same is true for their parents as well. The generation gap between you and your parents is much vast than ever before. Of course, these changes do not give parents the right to deal with the situation the way they like. Am I talking in your language here?? We all need to flow with the change. There has to be some logic and relevant 'yea' and 'nay' and not based on their upbringing.

Have you figured out what your parents dislike about you? Some of your minds just murmured – "They hardly like anything that I do!"

Hmm, but it does not work this way. Let us take up a thinking task and get going! There are a few things that are commonly disliked by almost all parents, for example:

- *Phone calls*
- *Watching television*
- *Mobile screen time*
- *Eating junk food*
- *Messy rooms*
- *Incomplete task*
- *Outing with friends*
- *Answering back*

This list can continue as you can add many more things out there.

Have you ever given deep thought to the reason why do these problems commonly exist with all parents? Have you not heard your friends having similar 'troubles' with their mom and dad?

You may try and convince your parents with the most basic argument, "No other parents do not object to anything, only you do!" But you very well know that the facts remain the same for everyone. Each one of you resorts to this same idea.

From the parent's point of view, the cases are a little different

Phone calls: What you view as simple phone-call they see the duration and exclaim them as long phone calls. They usually are long!

Watching television: Watching television is not an issue. Overtime of screen which leads to killing productive time is for sure a problem.

Mobile screen time: Mobile screen time is for sure about internet searches, project work, sharing notes which are required, we understand. Along with work time, you need time to chit chat and explore other apps as well, but within a limit. You extend time on Snapchat creating all those animal-faced pictures,

Plus making reels,

plus, watch YouTube DIY videos,

plus, click endless selfies for no reason,

plus, useless chats on WhatsApp,

plus, make video calls to kill time,

plus, going on a 'Musically or Spotify' spree too.

It is then you manage to pull their brain out of the box. This burial of your neck and mind in your mobile leads to the frying of parents brains.

Eating junk food: How can anyone have a healthy diet throughout the day and many days at a stretch? For sure, that sounds like a nightmare and no less than a punishment. But of course, your parents cannot let you spoil your health by being casual about it. They will not like to see Swiggy, Zomato, or Food Panda frequently ringing your doorbell, maybe almost every day.

Finally, eating junk food gets banned; sometimes, you resist ordering food. Whatsoever the case may be, you make sure to avoid the 'boring' home-cooked veggies by having Maggi or cuppa noodles at home. Unless dinner cooked is a fancy one, fried and spiced, noodles or home-baked pizza, you will not want to eat it once and for all. Once in a while, having outside food is acceptable. Check your frequency with the junk. I am sure you are grown up enough to be responsible, yeah? Parents will not want to see you digging into too much junk food, so there is a difference.

Incomplete task: Incomplete homework is possible due to ill health, excess of work with other genuine activities. But of course, undone homework can have no excuse at all. Being a student, the first important thing in your life is your daily routine work, while rest is secondary. Indulging in too much play leading to incomplete homework is injurious and certainly not acceptable.

Outing with friends: We all need to chill out with friends. Being with the buddies, laughing, sharing life's incidences are super stress busters! Parents do allow and happily let you go for birthdays or otherwise during the holidays. On the other hand, extra outings with no work done will prove to be a stress creator. You are most often chilling out while your work gets piled. Increased plans become a stress for parents, especially when exams knock at the door or grades are seen falling.

Answering back rudely: It is essential to reply to your parents. Of course, you need to respond to anyone who speaks to you, but politely. To answer without understanding the facts from others' points of view does not call for a healthy conversation at all. Honestly, whether you stand right or wrong becomes secondary if you hold a rude tone against parents or anyone else. There can be no reason to scream at them even if you have a valid point to prove yourself not guilty. Their focus will rightly get shifted to your rude attitude from the ongoing issue. There you land in trouble for answering back irrespective of your legitimate facts! You can politely deal with this one by keeping your breath calm and long. Go slow, take your own sweet time before you decide to answer back, do not puke out a whole lot of verbal garbage. Instead, be polite, have patience and give an ear to their thoughts and then explain. Do not allow the focus to shift to your 'tone' from the issue at hand.

While you are dealing with these situations your way, parents are equally facing them their way. They figure out that the only tool to bring your lost patience back is to command, "You are grounded"! They then stand as the most intolerant people, and it becomes the most hateful moment for you. Of course, you would not like it, will you? If not being grounded, your phone might get confiscated; you might be refrained from watching television or banned from meeting your friends and neighbours, and so on.

"Oh gosh! That is not the kind of life I deserve" could be your feelings which is obvious. But then why at all let the situations saturate to this level where you invite restrictions for yourself. You have the ability to change yourself and handle situations smartly, then why not utilise it and make life better. A deep secret is that even the parents do not like to give such punishments, but they are left no other choice. It is the most convenient way they find to imbibe the missing discipline in you.

They want you to have a 'real' social life, away from a virtual one, become independent, go out and meet people and learn to interact. They want you to use your grey matter as much as possible and do something constructive other than watching the idiot box, the television for the entire day. The excess screen time spent, like on the 'Snapchat' app, or while clicking random selfies, playing senseless online games, watching silly slime videos are acceptable for a short period only. Thus, no parent will like to see you repeat the same. All they see is that you are with a phone held in your hand. Trust that, after reading it, now you would not view your parents as autocratic as you considered at the beginning of this chapter.

PARENTS

You must read the contents from your point of view but understand things not as per your perception only. Let me be clear that the idea behind writing this book is to create a better understanding among both parents and the kids. Thus, the idea is that you must go through the points mentioned from the viewpoint of teenagers and understand them more deeply. It will help you take a plunge into their real life and will also fetch you chances to mend the ever-happening tiffs and rifts. You must peek into their mind, not with your mind but with a softer corner of your heart, and connect with them on a better emotional level. Try it out!

TWEENS &TEENS

When you read this book, try and look it from your parents' point of view. Try and understand who they are and where they come from (in their life). Just attempt to think of the situations from their perception, and you might conclude that they are not as illogical and unreasonable as you perceive them to be. Who knows, you might get your answers to nagging questions like -the reason why they stop you from going out on certain days. They ask you to spend time with your family instead. It is their way of dealing with things and how they look out for you.

One bright idea that just popped inside my head is about reading this book together. Why not mums, dads, and teens have a healthy read of this book over tea coffee each day? Find a convenient time for all and go page by page or a topic each day, or one chapter a day. Fifteen minutes or an hour can be spent on this book together every day, followed by healthy discussions. **Chapter 7 onwards begins the real story**. Share your views on the subjects in the book or even your ongoing issue of the day, if any. Let out your thoughts on this common open platform and clear your misunderstandings. It will help both of you to gain more insight, become peaceful and make better decisions! The micro irritants in both your minds are sure to vanish.

CHAPTER 3

THE TEEN TALK

Chinese is said to be the most difficult language, but you must have realised that the 'teen language' is not less difficult to adapt to. This ain't got anything to do with race or religion. Teenagers have a language of their own worldwide. To understand them better, deciphering their language is also very important. Well! In this way, you will connect better and prove yourself to be a modern parent fitting in their parameter of expectations.

While speaking to your teens, does it seem that you fail to understand their language, which is full of slang words, phrases and weird reactions? I doubt if you have had heard of these during your teenage. Times have changed and usage of such teen language among the teenage tribe is considered as a part of their developing self-esteem. It is also a sense of belonging for them.

Have a quick glimpse of the language which develops around the teenagers now. Over a chat - A simple 'Hello' becomes 'hiiee'; emphasising the repetition of alphabets indicates much excitement. While other ways of writing a simple hello include 'hiee...heyaa..'!

Mostly we all know the net speaks like lol, brb, ROFL, gtg which make up the terms of electronic communication, commonly known as chat language. Let me elaborate for the people who are not much aware. The acronym LOL stands for Laughing Out Loud; BRB – Be Right Back; ROLF- Rolling on The Floor Laughing; OMG – Oh My God; IDK – I don't Know; IDC – I Don't Care; GTG – Got TO Go; IKR – I know right; HAHA – This one goes without saying. And many more like these. *'Hey...how have you been...what is up with u today?'* or you can simply ask: *'Heyy... Sup?'*

They have their own innovative words or teen slang:

- *Lit – Cool, amazing*
- *Dope – awesome, cool*
- *Gucci – going well*
- *Bae – before anyone else*
- *Basic – boring, average*
- *Cap – Fake or lie*
- *No cap – no lies*

Likewise, there exist many words that make a kewl (cool) language altogether, where say 'peeps' stands for people, 'oki' stands for okay, and so on.

One of the happening words is 'mood'; another way of saying, "I agree"! By writing this, you actually do not have to mention it long "yes...so true..I know..that's correct...I second" you just write 'mood'. Telling that something is 'absolutely correct' is said to be a 'sure thing'!

Now next, your brother is your 'bro'. Mind it, not only your brother but also all your sister, even your friends are 'bro', both boys or girls.

Did you not get me? Oh! Bunk it then bro, I have no more clue about it.

One does not need to take the trouble of writing a complete sentence. Here I have a sample chat from my daughters' phone, which I have borrowed with due permission:

"Sup?"

'Your dp looks sesky bro... btw did you use the dog filter from Snapchat?

"Well! that's obvio man."

"So, you have been allowed Snap Chat... is it?"

"Yea...but shhh... pass (passcode) is known to Mommy."

"Okiii...that's kinda risky dude."

"I know bro. You are lucky as your confiscation stands due".

Communication

The above was a general chat between two friends. Aren't these people funny and have a weird style of talking? What do you think? Well, I tell you learning their language is far easier when it is about understanding them. Find your own way of communication to get a better understanding of them. But beware that you need to update yourself regularly as this language evolves rapidly.

Communication, discussion, and talks are of importance for everyone, especially for parents and teenagers. It helps to bridge the gap that prevails due to the difference in the mindset of both. Acceptance of others' points of view comes with communication which is a needed tool for a smoother life. You can enrich your relationships by simply talking your heart out without much delay.

All jokes apart, knowing their chat language is good fun. It is just another way of keeping the humour alive and helps build closeness.

Talking to them without judging on any of the matters;

discussing the topics that interest them;

understanding their views and opinions where it clashes with yours;

playing games of their choice; watching videos of their interest;

dancing & singing; listening to songs of their choice;

in simple words showing interest in their choice of activity will make each parent understand their kids better and share a happier life. Communication is the language for life that keeps relationships happy and healthy.

Teen slang is rapidly changing and is a normal part of the growing process. Parents must try and accept this as teens will constantly try to find several ways to keep their independence. Having a 'private' language between them and their tribe is one way of doing it. Well, this doesn't mean that you need to be excluded. In fact, it is your turn to let them know that you are willing to communicate in their language and interested in understanding their ongoing life.

Do not be judgemental, be someone who they can look upon for knowledge and guidance. And for this, you do not need to talk to them in their 'private language' ;)

CHAPTER -4

DESCRIBING A TEENAGER

How would you describe a teenager, regardless of whether you are among them or not!??

Parents View	Teens view
Temperamental	Trendy
Elusive	Easy
Energetic	Expressive
Naughty	Natural
Annoying	Adroit
Gauche	Gifted
Enigma	Expert
Restless	Radical

Thus, the description would vary according to the place from where you are looking at a teenager.

Here is my take on today's teens, what I see, and what I ought to see.

If you are a teenager, would you like to fit in or stand out?

Are you an Insta Junkie? or is the Snap chat string more like your thing?

Well, are you watching DIY videos or keeping up with the lyrics of the new numbers... either way, you are an honest Youtuber!

Being a teenager does not mean you follow the herd; you can be the trendsetter. It is necessary is to discover yourself. You should find out who you are as an individual? What are your leanings? and What do you want to become? But then, building up your individuality might seem tricky. Forming your own identity also might look like a difficult task. Reading good books like self-development books can help you to a great extent. Taking advice from people who have already experienced this stage of life in the recent past can be handy in building up your personality. You may even learn from your school seniors who excel in different fields. There can be many other people.

I would strongly recommend that you should not shy away from taking guidance from your School Counsellor. They are there to help you in all aspects and remove your doubts in all areas. Do not consider them to be there for 'special' kids only!

Well, firstly, before looking elsewhere for guidance, how about introspection?

Get a clear idea about the 'ideal self' you wish to have and must know your strengths and weaknesses to achieve the same. You also need not only to learn things but also to unlearn quite a few things.

Ways to understand yourself and bring about the needed changes in life:

1. Stay carefree, what we call a 'bindaas' attitude, and play the blame game!

Blame your parents, teachers, whoever you think are good for nothing. Be they your stupid professors, lousy neighbours, your rude bench mate, other cheesy friends, incompetent government, staff member, or anyone else. Take no responsibility for yourself and remain a victim. You can act like an animal - shout if you are hungry, scream when you are angry. Yell at your parents when they scold you for your good. If you feel like doing something and you know it is wrong or can prove hazardous, still do it.

Or be a responsible person and take charge of your actions.

2. Have no aim in life

Do not aim at doing anything productive no matter what. Do not make any goals for your studies, health, or otherwise. Never worry about the consequences of your actions or inactions. Sleep the whole day, watch television; Birthday parties must go on, outings must not stop, have five to six hours of screen time, and get completely wasted. You never know if you would be able to do all of these later, so why not keep the repeat mode on, not thinking about your future.

Or simply with the goal set and a clear road map, get going!

3.Put the necessary things in the pending folder.

Procrastinate perpetually! Do not take up the necessary things as a priority. The entire evening you can keep watching cricket match recaps;

keep chatting on Whatsapp or Snap; have endless conversations over the phone; watch DIY Youtube videos; listen to music in a blasting volume. Do not worry about your daily homework. Put off your incomplete work aside for tomorrow. Make sure that all the things that do not matter become your priority

Or make a daily list of "To Do" things and be sure to do the important ones on a priority basis.

4.Be unhappy about seeing the success of others.

Remember not to let your friends perform well by any means. See life as a competition and be jealous of the progress of others. If your friends win, it is a failure for you. In any case, you get a feeling that you are going to lose at the end, then drag that performing friend along with you to make sure he loses too.

Or maintain a positive attitude for everyone, including yourself, and be encouraged by the success of others.

5.Do not go for teamwork

People look weird to you only because they do and say things differently than you, isn't that true? You do not have to co-operate with them since your ideas will always be the best. Teamwork is meant for ants and bees then why to co-operate with mates. You think you are better off at performing things all alone, then why opt for a team? Stay aloof and remain a snob.

Or co-operate, collaborate, synergise and go for teamwork. Be your boss but take your team along.

6. Keep talking without listening

God has given you a mouth to speak, so why not keep talking and give a deaf ear to others? Express your side of the story, and only pretend to listen to others. Wait for them to understand your views without you trying to understand theirs. You can listen to their talk coldly and nod rudely, and even interrupt.

Or listen to people with an open mind. Trust me, listening to others is an art that one needs to develop more than speaking.

7. Never spend time on improving yourself

Time spent on improving yourself physically, mentally, and emotionally will be a total time waste. Do not learn anything new, do not care to study as you treat yourself over smart. Avoid keeping fit, eat loads of junk food. Just stay away from good books and good talks, and do nothing to motivate yourself.

Or keep yourself updated and renewed in all spheres.

8. Play the victim card

Keep grumbling about the things you fail to achieve. Blame your teachers for not giving enough marks, blame your staff for not working hard enough, blame your parents for not providing you enough resources, and so on.

Or stop passing the buck. Analyze and work for it.

If you want to change yourself, then do a simple activity. It is called 'mirror talk'! I'm sure you like to look at yourself in the mirror more than once during the day. We have a little add-on here, just that stand in front of the mirror, look into your eyes, and talk to yourself. Try and analyze what needs to change about you. Communicate to yourself, "Buddy, I do not like this thing about you; let us discard a bad habit and make space for a better one"! Do not expect quick results but keep trying. You will see a transformation in you which you might not have expected. Try out this Mirror exercise suggested by Louie Hay, and trust me, it is magical.

Always remember that your thoughts are stronger than you, and they even help you become even more resilient. Tune your mind to bring about the needed changes.

CHAPTER 5

HABITS

What are habits...any clue? If you ask me, habits are just actions on a repeat mode. You may not be completely aware of all your actions; they just happen without thinking. Habit is a practice that is hard to stop. You may not even realise about some of them unless somebody points them out to you. This is common for all. Habits can be both good and bad.

I read somewhere, "Habits do not change" despite our best efforts, some of it remains. *If you remove H from HABIT, A BIT still remains, remove 'A' and we have 'BIT', remove B, but 'IT' still remains.* Bad habits are tough to change because the Human brain does not really discriminate between the good ones and the bad ones. Most parents are anxious about getting rid of some of the bad habits in you. Do you think your parents are the same?

Bad habits usually pinch the nerve of parents. As a result of which the teenagers face adverse consequences! or is it the other way round? What do you say?

Most teens perceive their parents as dictators and are too much bugged with the typical perception parents hold about them in general and their habits in particular. In fact, they possess a 'habit' of correcting their children all the time. Habits tagged 'bad' by parents might actually not be so. We need to investigate further. Whatever the case may be, good habits are essential for both parents and teens.

Hey parents! from the moment your bundle of joy was born, you have always had a synchronised relationship. There was so much understanding and care. But if you feel it is not the same and things have taken a toll on your relationship, what exactly happened to that bonding? What went wrong? In these teen years, why haven't you guys been connected to each other in the same way?

Are these the 'habits' because of which things have changed between the two of you? Yes, this can be one of the reasons. What are the reasons you think that brought in bruises? Those unwanted dialogues, meaningless arguments, illogical tiffs have become a part of your life that never used to even exist before.

Today, as a mother, I am facing similar situations. I can absolutely relate to what my mother must have gone through during my teenage. Little here and a little there, we have all had teenage tantrums. I am now reliving my childhood days through my daughters, but the difference is that I am the mother this time (LOL). I can now understand my mother's apprehensions she then had.

It is quite possible that some of my good habits formed due to the beliefs embedded inside me as a child. I need to look at myself again and regularly check if those are still applicable to the kids of this generation. Times have been changing, and so are the beliefs. The parents of today might need a renewal of thoughts that can be done only by themselves. Peel away the layers of your old concepts and segregate the unwanted ones. Explore to discard those beliefs that are outdated. Eventually, you will have an updated notion about your children.

Habits – both good and bad

We all know habits are both good and bad. A few generalised good habits to have, are:

- Waking up early every morning
- Exercising daily
- Brushing your teeth both in the morning and at night
- Daily family communication
- Respecting others
- Planning your day/week/month as needed

- Limited screen time
- Reading

Oh! Come on, what am I talking about! How can one be so perfect and follow such a monotonous regime every single day? Some of you must be thinking that these talks sound good only in books. In fact, these are universally accepted good habits recommended for all ages, not really for teenagers only.

Teenage is said to be a crucial age when most of the bad habits get formed. It is thus known to be the foundation of character building. Let us now go into the detailing of different habits, or we can say lifestyle among the teens of today:

"2 more minutes, mommy!"

Two more minutes after mom wakes you up is the best sleep you could ever get, right? Oki, but mom asks how much can those two minutes practically satisfy your sleep hunger? Also, do you actually get out of the bed after two minutes, or do you make it twenty? Do you keep sleeping and wait for your mom's cringy voice to wake you up again in about half an hour or maybe more?

Apart from sleep issues, other commonly used dialogues these days go like this:

"All my friends have it, and so I also need it."

"All my friend's parents have allowed for the outing, only you say no to everything."

"Mum, chill! I shall do it sometime later."

"I'm okay with a dirty room. Please don't bother mum!"

"I will be done with my assignments; please don't worry."

"I need a boyfriend! I feel out of place when my classmates talk about their"

"Permit me Netflix series; all my friends are allowed to watch."

"Can I watch a movie please" (just before the exams)

"I shall set my routine in the morning."

"No mum, no green veggies, give me Maggie instead!"

"All you can do is just ban my phone."

"Mum, you have become so mean these days."

"Oh! Mum, please don't overreact..."

As these issues are universal so why not discuss them with friends and cousins of your age? Find a solution to these everyday squabbles. I do believe that most of these issues would simply disappear by following a disciplined and healthy regime.

Parents and Diary

About myself

Let me share something about my writing habit. I used to write diaries to note down all my complaints. I also noted my stress; my fights; my likes and dislikes, my happy moments too. Writing about my daily affairs about friends, teachers, neighbours had become a regular practice, and soon my diary became my companion. Despite having a diary to share my feelings with, there could be no better companion than my parents. They have always been my friends and guide. Mom did raise her eyebrows, screamed, had hot flushes of anger, there were restrictions, I got scolded too and more. Yet, they have always remained my best friends. After years when I look at myself today, I am so thankful for what I have been moulded into, and I still need them the same way. No matter I have grown much older and have two teen kids of my own, but I know that there can be no better guide than them.

Back to the diary

Back to dairy, it is indeed a good habit to write one. My experience tells, that to be able to pen-down your feelings and also to share them with your parents is the best combination. Diary will absorb everything you write and will be good to read and enjoy later but will not reciprocate. You can fill as many diaries as you want; they can only be your punch bag. They can de-stress you but can never become your guide.

Diary cannot teach you life lessons;

it will not correct your mistakes;

it will not make you realise your weaknesses;

it will neither laugh with you at your jokes nor will it console you at your lows, unlike your parents.

Mom and Dad shall remain the best guides for your lifetime, so mix-match to deal with situations. I believe writing creates clarity in your thoughts, thus helping you interact better with them.

There is another way to look at this. You, as a teenager, can write your views in your personal diary, which can also be a medium to fill the communication gap between you and your parents. While you express your feelings in words, your mom and dad can read the same and understand you better. This can avoid heated arguments. Unnecessary tiffs can definitely bring better and quicker solutions than otherwise.

I know that you may have your share of 'secrets' that you would not like to reveal. But at the same time, if you feel the need to share a suggestion, but hesitate to speak, so why not write a 'tell all' note to your parents and seek advice? Just as was done by Mahatma Gandhi when we wrote to his dad, confessing his guilt of theft and eating meat.

And now you know that if you hesitate to speak about some stuff, you can make writing your medium and convey your message simply to them, bingo!

Now parents have to definitely go through the diary pages with an open mind. This reading of the diary needs to be an important task and dealt with velvet gloves. Both of you may sit together discussing 'coolly' the already noted down points in it.

Similarly, an improvised version of the same idea says that both mum and teens can maintain their diaries separately. Write down your perceptions about the ongoing issue, and then sit together for idea exchange about each problem. This diary exchange can gradually help you put yourselves in each other's shoes and see things unbiased. As you both read each other's perceptions, you shall get a clearer picture of the entire episode. In this way, communication can be made deeper and better. This is indeed a good solution sorter that excludes high pitch voices, rude tones, misunderstandings, high pulse rates, arguments, irritation, negativity, and more.

This is my idea about writing and understanding, but, as a teen, you might not agree with me. A teenager might feel the following manner:

Wait, why at all a diary? Why does a Diary have to be my companion when I have my friends to talk to? There could be a million reasons why people like to write diaries, but I am not one of them! I have my best friend to take care of all my troubles. Similarly, I shall lend my ears to hear her out whenever needed.

Kids please do not believe me blindly on the solutions, only because I have written them down as suggestions. I insist that you must try them out and then conclude yourself. Do not be in a hurry.

Few advantages of writing a diary that has quickly come to my mind are:

1. It is an outlet for your emotions.
2. It is the safest area to pour your heart out without confronting anyone.
3. It improves your communication with yourself. As you pen down your thoughts, you get a clear picture of what exactly you want.
4. It helps you read and re-read your thoughts even later in life.
5. It can help you rationalise your thought when you read it the next time in a better mood.
6. You can write things without hesitations which otherwise would be difficult to speak out.
7. Express your feelings without any interruptions. Be it your anger or excitement.

8. It can help you explore your past. Parents can relive your childhood now, teens you too can enjoy reading these issues later in life.

9. You can learn from the diary by re-reading it time and again.

10. It can be your happy place absolutely, your solitude where you can meet yourself and explore your emotions calmly.

There can be many more.

This is true and proven that once you write down your feelings, you know what you want. You will have a processed idea about yourself. You can dig deeper into your emotions to explore what exactly troubles you. It will help you rationally think and decide rather than jumping to a hasty conclusion, which otherwise leads to a conflict. Both mums and teens will be able to redefine their arguments and gain a win-win situation for both.

I am taking a step towards writing down my feelings and perception of the teens on similar matters. My daughters shall be for sure my guiding light for the portions of the teen life they deal with. Situations, problems, and solutions can differ from family to family, place to place, person to person, and age to age. You may find different solutions to the similar issues discussed in this book. Do share your ideas with me; I would love to hear your opinion about the same problems. Discussions are always healthy.

In the upcoming chapters, let us deal with a few of the situations in common, which I'm sure every parent and teen goes through. This book will help mainly mums explore their kids' teen-hood with a different perspective. Teens also may find better answers to some of their questions. Hey teenagers! It is a golden opportunity for you to peek into the hearts and minds of your parents.

CHAPTER -6

MUM-TEEN PROBLEMS

I am writing this Chapter to prepare both the sides, parents and teens, to enter each other's realm and experience both perspectives. It will help them realise what goes on in there, kind of a reality show through hidden cameras.

There have always been problems big or small between mums and their growing muffins. The rationale behind any situation is that it becomes a problem only when it is unwelcome or disapproved by either side. A problem is 'just a trivial issue' for the teens, whereas, for mums, problem spells 'trouble'!

Some of the most common issues to be dealt with are:

Cleanliness & hygiene | time management | academic performance | the wrong food habits | value for money | adolescence | peer pressure | career confusions | emotional imbalance| outings, and plans |

When we tag the problems as challenges, it is then we find their solutions. These terms sound like 'big issues'; but trust me, these are merely small challenges that we can overcome easily. They are not always complicated. But yes, delayed communications often make them impenetrable and tough to handle.

Not all problems require much discussion; there would be no need to deal with each one of them by the diary process. There exist many simple challenges that will sort out in the blink of an eye. They usually seem big than they actually are. Since challenges keep occurring on a repeat mode, you need to work on breaking their cycle.

In 'The Tricky Teens' let us pick one challenge at a time. As a mum, I have written my part of the story. I have done the same on behalf of the teens, after a vision input from my daughters' point of view! After all, they are my co-authors, and it would not be possible to turn this manuscript into a book without their version. In a way, Camera 1 shall focus on Parents and Camera 2 on Teens.

I have recalled instances from my personal journal and have quoted stories of some other mothers too. Both my daughters have helped me by sharing their ideas and perspective on the same. You, I and everyone else shall be able to relate to each other's issues as we mostly sail in the same boat.

One takeaway which is common to all the issues between parents and teens is:

Timely and proper communication between the two can resolve most issues before they turn into trouble for both! I wish it remains etched on the minds of both.

Between the Mom & Teen Duo

In the following chapters, I have put my best efforts into showcasing both sides of the story. Stay tuned as we move on to the most talked about topics between the duo 'mum and teen'.

CHAPTER 7

CLEANLINESS

MOM's side of the story

The weekend is the time which everyone looks forward to, I too so do. The entire week passes by doing the daily chores. A routine life comes to a recreational break after five days of the daily grind. Ah! Saturday is a day to relax. We all have our own definitions of relaxation. It could be dinner, drive, movie, coffee time, fun with friends and other near and dear ones, catching up with old connections, and making new ones.

Like many other people, Saturday is a day for completing all my piled-up housework. I find myself some extra time for content writing since the following day is a holiday. I also look forward to making pending social calls and to me-time reading and surfing. But this particular Saturday was a special one. I had a panel discussion to attend at the Women's Writers Fest, where I was invited as one of the panellists. How thrilling! This was going to be my first such experience with 'She the people. TV', so the excitement was too high for sure. I made sure to finish my morning regime along with some extra work. Everyone had to manage by themselves as I would be away. I was too late to even wake kids up to begin their day. I wanted to make it a little ahead of time than my scheduled panel. It was an interesting discussion about 'self-publishing' where I happily spoke about my journey of my debut book 'Bee Magical'. It was an absolutely gratifying day. I met many people who appreciated my book. To be introduced as an author was a new experience altogether. The place gave me feelings of inspiration and joy as I made many new connects.

I returned home in the evening after this long and happy day, enjoying my afterthoughts of the wonderful time I had. It was happily tiring to keep standing and greeting new people out there. I was desperately seeking to stretch myself on my bed. Our house help was away, but how much I wished to be served a cup of hot coffee. With coffee on my mind, I opened the door of the house with my set of keys. I wondered what went wrong out here. Any guesses what I saw as I entered home?

Gosh! The entire house was a mess! It was utter chaos and such an unclean place, so much so that it brought the feeling of a railway platform. Sorry to say, but that is how we denote a dirty area in India.

What would be your feelings about the house which is seen with carelessly opened shoes and sandals strewn across maximum space in front of the shoe rack? There were discarded candy wrappers thrown around, unfolded newspapers swaying in fan breeze trying to reach the corners of the walls.

I stepped forward and found a wet towel from the shower still waiting on the couch. It must have dried under the fan by then. The lunch dishes were lying on the table, screaming to be soaked in the kitchen sink, the television was noisily on, and there was no one to even watch it. The schoolbags stacked on the chair still contained the previous day's lunch box, and bottles were peeping out from the side pockets.

This entire scenario was testing my patience. I dreaded to think what I would find when I enter their room. I don't need to mention who I am talking about! I finally entered their room, you know what, it looked as if recently hit by a hurricane. No, I am not exaggerating!!! Now let me tell you why.

The school uniform was discarded on the floor. A dirty hairbrush lay full of hair strands was on the bed. School badge and identity card were sighted on the bedside table. There were empty juice cans (crushed mercilessly) lying on the floor, and drops of juices around them was a meal for the ants. This isn't all. The cupboard was wide open as if displaying the messed-up shelves, a sling bag hanging on its handle, and a pack of tissue lying opened on the edge of the bed. Almost all clothes from the cupboard had been stacked on the bed. (It is a familiar scene when going to a party). I wonder why one needs to pull out all the clothes to decide on a particular one to be worn? Why can't one find it easier to choose from neatly piled up clothes on the shelves instead; any clue?

Besides all of this, the books were mostly scattered around the room. Corners of the room and the window niche are permanent places for the pile of books. I don't know why we bring them fancy desks to study, and why at all do they have separate study rooms (in many houses).

Next, I do not want to even discuss the bathroom in detail. Yuk scene with sticky shampoo bottles and the soap that floated in its personal swimming pool case. Let's just bunk details!

The first impression of the house had already had my temper high while this room raised it further. I tried my best to stay calm and not scream my lungs out at the 'monsters'. I reminded myself again that I have to respond and not react. There walked in the partners in crime – Tiara and Anya.

 "Who did this all?" was my spontaneous question though I already knew the answer; it was something foolish to ask. My younger one was smart enough to quietly leave the room without a word. "Could you not be responsible enough to keep your room clean" was my next question. I had not expected an apology because it generally does not come. I received a retort instead, "It is not the first time you have seen a dirty room. Chill mom," With this Tiara too left the room as if it was a trivial matter and needed no discussion.

Firstly, the mess with no guilt, no apology, followed by the retort, then her moving out in attitude, frustrated me. Can't I expect anything better? It was a usual thing for me to feel such remorse. I tried to calm my nerves down but somehow failed to do it. I happened to walk after her with a cleanliness tirade. I angrily accused her of messing up the house, told her this is what her younger sister was indirectly learning from her. I narrated to her stories; how organised I used to be even during my school days, how I used to keep my books and clothes neatly piled up and in place. The lengthy lecture did not affect her and seemed to slip like water down a duck's back. I strongly feel that kids do not have value and gratitude for the things they own. She wasn't even a bit affected, and it made no difference to her; Rather, it was me who was just helplessly poured my anger on her. I went on with my lecture, and there followed more of my pent-up emotions that got an outlet right there and then.

I paused because I was drained both mentally and physically. With a feeling of complete exhaustion, I laid down on the bed, took a deep breath, and closed my eyes to calm myself. I had lost my cool absolutely.

Tears rolled down my cheeks as I realised, though not unreasonably, I had scolded her more than required. After a great day, the sight of the dirty house had taken a toll on me. I lost my cool more because of other things that had piled up in the past many days, but all pent-up emotions burst out on her alone. The Saturday that I had expected to be happy and an exciting one actually ended up in anger, irritation, and tears.

Suddenly I smelled a revitalising aroma; I opened my eyes to a relieving sight. My dolls stood right there with a cup of hot coffee and cookies served on a tray. Oh my, my... the little devils stole my heart once again, with their care they affection and left me speechless. Motherly love took over me, and I felt mixed emotions of guilt and love. I hugged them both and told them how desperately I wished for a cup of hot coffee but was too tired to even make it.

I was now pretty sure that I should have calmed myself down before scolding her, and that would have ended the day on a much better note. We cuddled & kissed, making it all brighter and better.

After receiving the energy-boosting cuddle and having coffee, I helped her clean the entire mess to make up for the rebuke. In a way, it was my apology to her without saying it in words. Seeing a grin on her face, I was sure my vibes had travelled to her. My only regret was that I forgot to even ask her about how her day went and what happened in the school drama selection.

Just curious to know how would your mother react to a messy state of the house like this, especially after a happy yet hectic day?

Cleanliness

TEEN side of the story

It was Saturday morning... I woke up all by myself today without snoozing my alarm clock. Mum did not have to wake me up like all other days. I was feeling alive and energetic and did not wish to laze around today. Wow! What a great feeling indeed. You know why because it wasn't any ordinary Saturday, it was the one I had been looking forward to past many days. I had my auditions for the annual show in my school, followed by more fun during the day.

I quickly got ready, had my breakfast. Mum had left early, so I did all my stuff by myself. Although I had to reach later than the usual school timing, we took off a little ahead of time. Dad dropped me at school and took Anya along with him. Many others reached early due to the 'obvio' excitement in all of us. We had a great time rehearsing our dialogues and practicing actions. At the end of the audition...Guess what? I was selected for the role I wanted to enact (read a grin)! Yay! What a great start to the day.

Next came the outing with friends that we had already planned. Exams were over, so we all had permission to hang out today. We went to a movie all by ourselves, there were no parents or elders with us. One of my friends had managed her car to pick us up one by one from our homes. We all were thrilled to go back, change our clothes, have lunch, and rush as per the movie timing.

I reached home, took the house key from our next-door neighbour. I tried to get ready quickly, opened my cupboard, and pulled out clothes to find the pair of blue denim I was looking for. I stacked them all on the bed in a hurry but did not have time to neatly put them back in. Anyways that was not important to do at that hour. I put on my jeans and white hoodie that made me look the best. I had to hunt for the hairbrush as Supriya di (our house help) was away, and there was no one else to keep things back in place. I looked around the room and found empty cans on the floor, but that is not all. A few books lay here and there, and wrappers of energy bars swayed. Empty packets of chips and dairy milk chocolate danced under the fan, all thanks to the midnight snacking the previous night! Gosh! Mom would kill me if she was here right now. Asking Anya for help once she would be home with Dad made no sense as she would say, "Do it yourself!" Anyways, I found the hairbrush. Probably I had thrown on the bed while hurrying in the morning, quickly brushed my hair, pulled out a wet tissue napkin, and neatly wiped my face to look fresh and clean. I was done, I guessed.

But no wait, I was supposed to eat lunch as well. Mum had prepared my fav Baked Rice before leaving, and I must have it. I hurried into the kitchen and served myself some rice. There wasn't any time to warm it as my friends would reach any moment to pick me up.

I was gobbling my lunch sitting on the couch when I heard a car honking. I was absolutely on time to finish my last bite. I quickly wiped my hand with the same tissue that I had wiped my face with, picked up my sling bag, and moved towards the door. My footwear??!! I emptied a few of the pairs from the top shelf of the shoe rack to look for my sneakers and found them at the backside. I carefully locked the house and handed back the keys to our friendly neighbours. Even though I had no cape I felt like a super girl while moving towards the car. I had managed to get ready on time without wasting a single moment. Huh! A sigh of relief and satisfaction.

I returned home after roars of laughter and fun, we enjoyed a good comedy movie. I eagerly wanted to share my wonderful day with Anya as soon as I reached home. She waited for me desperately as she had been bored the entire day. I had got her a pack of chips just to compensate for my absence. No matter how much we fight, she is my little sis' after all. Very happy to see me, she hugged me with excitement. By the way, I know her excitement was more for the pack of chips and not me (please read a tongue-out emoji here). Of course, dad had come back home too. We jumped inside mom's bedroom; I could not wait to tell them about my day from the very beginning. Dad was excited to know that I was selected, and he promised me a treat after the final show. I enacted my part in the room as they clapped for me. It was so much fun! I was eagerly waiting to repeat my performance before mom.

Suddenly we heard some faded noises coming from outside, so we went to check out what had interrupted our giggles.

From here, you already know what happened. Right? No! not everything, I guess. It was none other than mommy. I expected her to enquire about my school audition and outing, but it did not happen. She was scandalised seeing the messy house and began with her not so uncommon ranting. While mom was not really screaming her lungs out on me but her agitation was high and could be made out from her expression. Probably her invisible anger had risen so much so that we could bake a pizza on her head, she might have screamed any moment. Our dad stood there as if trying to give us a warning with a weird look which hinted me to remain calm. Obviously, he messes up his room and knows how to deal with mom (Lol). I cautiously stood there without moving or uttering a word while mom gave me a killing look. I knew I was about to be hit with a tsunami of words right away. I was proved correct as mom started with her barking lecture to me. The funny thing she asked was, "Who made the mess?". OMG! Obvio it's me, doesn't she know that? I was kind of laughing within as today's excitement had not died. I could not hold myself back even after dad's warning. Did not know what to say, unprepared I just uttered that it is not the first time she had seen such a messed-up room. My words added fuel to the fire, and she lost it on me absolutely.

A few chocolate wrappers are no harm if seen around the house; does it really matter, dude? Cans are supposed to be crushed! When crushed, they cannot be kept on the bed for sure, and the books obviously wouldn't lay there for the entire term, right. Oh, she and her overreactions! Okay...okay... I know that rooms shouldn't be kept so messy. The fact is that the room actually looked as if it was my turn in the game of Jumanji, but then I did not really find time for cleaning up, you know. But no, she wouldn't give me a chance to open my mouth to speak up, so it was better to actually leave the room, although it did backfire me, that's a different story.

Finally, she went to her room, and hence we all got a breather. It was quiet as the silence after the storm. I somehow realized that her scolding was justified but not that severe. Like us, mom had a long day too! We with dad sat down looking at each other and thinking what to do...what could uplift mum's mood...mum was exhausted, so we exactly knew what to do. A hot cup of coffee! Coffee was not only our saviour, but it also fetched us tight hugs and kisses in return. She even helped me clean the mess!

Whatsoever, the only lesson I need to learn is that come what may, just keep your room clean and head cool!

P.S: Guys, Stay organised. Be compassionate.

CHAPTER 8

LATE AND LAZY

Late and lazy by mom

What do you think an alarm clock does? Yes, it is designed to alert people about a specific time. Its primary function is to wake people up after a good night's sleep or after short naps.

Not only kids but also people in general use the alarm function on their mobile phones. I prefer the use of alarm clocks, especially for the kids, so that they can peacefully switch off their phones and keep them away from their beds. Phones are a complete distraction and do not allow timely sleep.

Kids have their own alarm clock and a backup too that has all the functions. It is always in good working condition but, mind you, more than the alarm function, snooze works in it the best. Mobile snooze too simply get activated by voice command: "Hey Siri, stop the alarm". After the snooze function of the alarm clock gives up.

The backup alarm, universally used by kids, is of the "Mom" brand! I need to check up on them to make sure that they are out of bed. As usual, the snooze command from Tiara comes, "Two minutes, please!" but believe me, these two minutes continue even after twenty minutes or more. I must say, Anya never asks for these two minutes. It is not because she wakes upon being called but because she knows she will automatically get this extra time because of her elder sister. So why even make an effort to respond to mom's wake-up call.

Somehow, this is the usual start to my days, and this happens quite often. Unwillingly, I am forced to grumble every morning, which is quite irritating.

I am writing about one such morning when the alarm rang as per the set time. But since snooze works better, so the chance of kids remaining asleep was high. I entered their room and found them sleeping. Pillows had been abandoned, and blankets were tucked-in from all sides; after all, who would bother to even switch off the AC. My calling out to them did not work, so I had to shake them up. Anya clinged to Tiara and cleverly managed to investigate with her barely opened eyes, just to make sure that she was sleeping. This gave her the license to stay in her place unmoved. After some time, I was there calling out to them once again. Tiara opened her eyes to see me standing over her head. She gave me an unpleasant look, and without any exchange of dialogue, she got out of the bed and slammed into the washroom. I am sure she can break the world record (if any) of having a shower in the shortest time ever. Anya lazed on the bed, enjoying her extra minutes till Tiara came out. They managed to dress up and also collect their books from the corner of the room to arrange them in their school bags. Of course, the timetable was not set the previous night.

All this time, I waited at the table for them with their breakfast, lunch boxes, and their water bottles. They finally opened their room, and the entire hall freshened up with a floral fragrance. God knows how quickly they can get ready with everything done within less than even ten minutes. Tiara came hurriedly just to stuff her mouth with breakfast of 'baked beans on toast. It took her hardly a couple of minutes to finish it, leaving a bite at the end, which seems more like a ritual. People leave a bite before beginning their food as their offering to God. But with them, this ritual comes with a twist. Anyways, it is always indifferent with Anya when it comes to food. She had little less choice in food and hence gulped down 'Pediasure' milk and was done with. There was no time left for her to eat because Tiara had headed towards the lift by then. With her socks in hand to be worn in the car and no exchange of a pleasant smile, she ran into the lift saying, "Hurry up! Anya, bye mom." Anya followed her.

They run a marathon almost every morning. I wonder what happened to those kids who used to get ready ahead of time, who used to sit peacefully to finish their breakfast while I used to calmly plait their hair. I sat brooding why at all was this happening? How did I fail to keep their childhood habits alive? Habits like setting up their school bag at night, and also of waking on time? Why are they not particular about peacefully eating their breakfast before leaving home? Why did they give up their habit of giving a minute to saying their morning prayer? I contemplated that the mornings are troublesome to wake up Tiara, while Anya mostly copied her. So, if at all I could put her into a regime once again, Anya would automatically follow. This morning marathon had been quite regular for a few months, and probably the reason was late bedtime. I mostly found Tiara awake till late because she read her favourite novel or tried to finish her pending TV shows. This was another reason why I had been sulking this morning.

The absence of a smile on my face and my continuous frowning lastly helped them to wake up on time for the next few days. They also set their school bag at night and made sure that they do not have to do that in the morning.

No one knows better than me how I wish to hug them each morning and peacefully sit with them to exchange a few happy moments and smiles before they would leave for school. Who at all wants to begin the day with grumbles and fights? And ruin it for themselves and for the others? Not me!

Does your mom ruin your day like this too? I'm sure you know that you have the key to stop her grumblings, which is very simple indeed.

Late and Lazy

Better defined as Triple time action by Teens'

Morning alarm sucks! Can you tell who has not Snoozed alarms, be it on the clock or the phones? I am sure we all have done it. Snooze function has been given to snooze, or else why would it be there at all? Who can explain this to mommy, not me at least! She had told me, that earlier there used to be alarm clocks that had no snoozing option, so obviously, how would people snooze! How!? More so, mom wants me to sleep latest by 10 pm. Who at all sleeps so early, I wonder, when there is much to do! Anyways, getting back to the alarm, don't even ask about those extra five minutes that we get during the snooze, but that seems to be our birth-right! Believe me, in those few minutes, it feels like getting an extra night of sleep.

Sharing my experience below:

It was like any other day when I had to hurry. Woke up late because I had slept late. Snooze was on, and I kept sleeping.

Let me tell you what actually happens when you hit the snooze button thinking that you shall wake up in the next five minutes. You actually tend to travel in a different zone altogether. Your subconscious mind takes you on to the most peaceful journey like never before until you get those dinosaurs kind of trembling in your body. It is nothing but your mother shaking you to wake you up. Am I right? And then you realise that the five minutes you wanted to sleep more has taken away all your time. You are now left with only five minutes in hand to absolutely finish off all the tasks, from waking up to crashing into the car.

I did not find time to have a bath which I usually do not take (who would bathe before going to school ya), so to keep myself fresh, I sprayed deodorant instead. I filled my pocket with some chewing gums (Shh... I did not get time to even brush my teeth, I have got braces bro', so chewing gum is a must to keep them clean.). Loaded my school bag with the books I could lay my hands on. I gobbled my breakfast unwillingly and then hurried out with half-worn shoes and socks in my hand. Finally, both Anya and I sat in the car. I popped in a piece of gum to keep my breath fresh. Radio channel 93.5 FM was playing, we sang along the latest numbers till we reached school. As I entered school guess what? I suddenly remembered the homework that I had absolutely forgotten about. I got so engrossed in my novel at night that doing homework had just slipped out of my mind. What seemed unimportant yesterday that I kept procrastinating was actually important. This realisation came to me as usual at the last moment.

I then tried to figure out who to borrow the graph paper from? I had forgotten to carry that also. As I neared the classroom, I also got reminded of the maps my geography teacher had asked us to submit today. Oh no! I had to hurry up as I was already getting late for the assembly, else I would be punished in front of all.

I cannot just go on writing each and every detail, so let me just jump forward to the end of the day and tell you the highlights. So, the school was boring as usual. Other than the lunch that we secretly had during the active history period much before the break. And ya, how can I forget to tell you that I luckily escaped scolding for my homework because my teacher was absent? I managed the graph paper from a friend, but doing the maps was additional work for me because I had forgotten my completed maps at home. I must confess that I had a tough time standing outside my class' in the English period as I had not carried my book. I was even scolded by my Physics teacher, in front of my classmates, for being irresponsible. I wasn't allowed to share the Physics book. I felt terrible! We were soon dispersed.

While coming back home in the car, I sat thinking about the disappointing day that had gone by. I promised myself to set my routine at night and go to bed on time, just to escape these embarrassments and harassment in school. Not setting up my timetable the previous night and snoozing the alarm had actually cost me this day.

I reached back home and had a shower without wasting time. I had lunch and relaxed for a while. Then sat with my home task and pending work of the previous day; I completed them taking short breaks. By evening I was free to go down and play with my neighbourhood friends. I even got time to catch my favourite TV show late in the evening. My bag was ready and kept in the hall after putting in all the needed things for the next day. My novel was my companion when I finally hit the bed around 10pm. It was not that tough to be organised as it otherwise seemed. The next day the only thing that I looked forward to was my Mum, my most reliable alarm, to wake me up. Actually, I do not trust my alarm clock; it snoozes a lot, you see! (Please read a winking emoji here ;))

Hope we all understand right here that all we need to do is sacrifice the extra time that we take at night. Guys, change your sleeping time, read your novel at a different hour, use that time to set your routine instead. Chat to your friends in the day. In any case, you haven't understood yet, then I wish you all the strength to face your mom's frown every morning. God can only save you, or maybe your dad.

CHAPTER 9

ADOLESCENCE

Adolescence comprises various changes in the body, which include physical, mental, and biological. While hitting the stage of puberty, the children are like:

- *"I don't feel like eating"*
- *"I don't feel like talking."*
- *"Please leave me alone!"*
- *"I feel like I am going to die."*
- *"Sorry about what I said earlier; I did not mean it that way."*
- *"Life is always unfair with me."*
- *"I need some junk food."*
- *"Am I looking dark today?"*
- Etc, etc...

These are some dramatic dialogues with added expressions said by them (you know who I mean). Their appropriate nasty expression, tone, and pitch sound as perfectly as delivered by actors in films!

Well, the contents of this chapter can be hazardous. This is a statutory warning, so later, do not say that I did not warn you.

Welcome to the danger zone, which is far more menacing than the areas with lava-spewing volcanoes.

I was in anxiety when she frantically rushed out of the bathroom and came to me crying with a puppy-like expression. I feared the worst of the puberty phase (yes, the monthly cycle), but no, it wasn't so. She stood there silently, pointing at her face. Somehow, I failed to figure out what exactly she was trying to show till she lost her patience. In anger, she brought her face much closer for me to get an enlarged view of the invisible problem on her cheek and screamed, "Look what has happened." My anxiety then eased, realising that she was upset with something on her skin. As I already wear lenses, I doubted my eyesight. Had my sight gone worse since this one was actually challenged by vision? With some extra effort, I finally figured out the tiniest red dot that had newly visited her cheek.

Yes, for my daughter, it was a shock much bigger than a volcanic eruption when she saw the first out- burst of a tiny red spot on her face. We usually call it 'pimple', but to her, it seemed something unique being witnessed for the first time on this planet!

I resisted laughter, but it burst out naturally. The louder version wasn't because of this tiny red thing. In fact, it was due to the peace I felt putting aside the puberty issues for the time being. I realised Tiara wasn't finding it hilarious at all. I held her because she was sad. I felt as if she had lost all her beauty, and her world had come crashing down. I advised her not to use anything artificial on her face to cover the red thing else it might grow and spread. These days a direct 'NO' does not work, which used to till a couple of years back. They now needed patience and explanation, a bit cajoling, and more.

Though the entire scene of pimple drama was over, I realised that she still looked tensed the same way. On talking further, I came to know that I had missed the real problem. The actual problem wasn't the pimple, but it was her friends who might tease her on seeing it. (I thought how would they at all see it unless she showed it to them with a magnifying glass). That was not all; her next worry was that her friends who had acne would now tease her since she had made fun of them in the past. The very next moment, I heard her murmuring to God as she pleaded to let this be her last time; she would never ever pull anyone's leg for their looks and problems. Good, I thought to myself, this was a lesson she needed about not making fun of others.

At the same time, I wanted to know her friends' reactions in the school. I waited for her and was happy to see her return home with a smiling face. No one pulled her leg; it was a healthy day. She understood that pimples are just a part of adolescence and sooner or later hits almost everyone. It was nice self-realisation that smiling was the best option to cover the imperfections on her face. I was happy and remembered the days when similar things had happened to me too as a teenager.

Adolescence

or we can say 'Moods' by teens!

It is just before sleeping that I look into the bathroom mirror every day. Now don't ask me why; I just do that to smile at myself, appreciate how beautiful God has made me, and I like it. The reflection of me brings me happiness and gives me a peaceful. Today was a dreadful experience altogether when I stood before the mirror to exchange a smile. I was taken aback by the look on the other side. I was shocked to see the most visible red dot sitting on my cheek like a king. It was right there distinctly seen. I screamed by default and did not know how to help myself. I then looked carefully at my entire face. Thankfully rest was all okay. I checked twice before confirming that to myself. I knew I needed help for the newly erupted volcano-like pimple. I was on the verge of crying, but I consoled myself, saying that it was the first-ever that happened to me and thus my friends might not tease me. With teary eyes, I rushed out of the bathroom to mom for the best advice on this.

I found her right there waiting for me to come out after hearing my scream. I don't have to describe how much effort it took me to actually explain my problem to her. She literally laughed at something which had filled me with dread, how insensitive and unkind. She kept laughing, ignoring my feelings absolutely. She seemed to prove that she had the worst eyesight ever; she could not see this red thing that highlighted my cheek. She asked me if I was actually showing her any problem, I confidently answered 'yes' without even losing a moment. She probably then considered that I actually had a problem.

I then had to work hard and indirectly ask for her compact powder to apply before going to school to hide it. She immediately said a strict no for it giving her own reasons. When at all does mom understand this kind of a crucial problem? Fine, I had to face it!

I entered my school and also my classroom with this hill on my cheek. I sat down quietly, trying to hide the pimple-side away from people. These things are very easily noticed by the teens, I guess. We have the vision of a hawk; anyways, it was not so bad in the school. My friends did not really make fun of me. We all played as we usually do and had fun as on any other day. They were kind enough to take my tiny volcano coolly despite me making fun of them when they had it. I felt comfortable, confident, and relieved.

The lessons I learned from my mom and certain friends about this pimple and acne were:

Do not make fun of other peoples' looks.

These are not just limited to girls; these mini volcanoes erupt on boys as well.

One must have 10-12 glasses of water every day to flush out toxins. Eat less junk food just for the time being, so you don't have to quit it for long.

Keep your face and head clean because germs from dandruff, etc., can get you pimples and acne.

PS: By the way, Aloe Vera, sandalwood, and fuller's earth are a few of the best natural cures for acne, pimples, and scars.

CHAPTER -10

PEER PRESSURE

The hallmark of adolescent experience!

Pressure Cooker! Why pressure cooker? One can either cook tasty food in it or mishandle it, and it can blow up, causing great harm. Use peer pressure judiciously, and it may help you serve a deliciously cooked meal on life's platter. You use it indiscriminately, it may blow up in your face causing severe damage, at times irreversible.

What is peer pressure? 'Peer' comes from the Latin word par, meaning equal. When you socialise with people of similar age, having similar interests, or backgrounds, you are involuntarily affected by their behaviour. Their attitude, or habits, also convince you to do certain things. You are then said to be under peer pressure. By the way, this pressure cooker of life does not exist in teenagers alone. Most certainly, we have all experienced it at some time or the other with our peers.

Peer Pressure is both bad and good and usually taken negatively. It is harmful when you get influenced by it and good when it inspires you.

When you feel peer pressure and act prudently, it can prove to be good for you. You need to be alert to warning signals, just as the pressure cooker whistles when the pressure increases unduly, and take corrective action. If your BFF chooses Economics, that does not mean that you should too. You may be good at literature so do not feel pressurised to follow your friend. There may be people in your peer group who are into smoking or drinking or regular late-night outs, which are harmful not only for your health but also for your career. This teenage period of life is a sensitive phase, and one must know the difference between bad and good. Also, one must have the courage to say no to such pressure from peers. This ability to tell 'NO' to 'bad and unwanted' is one takeaway I insist you have from this chapter.

Other than bad habits, there is another aspect to negative peer pressure: Owning the latest gadgets! When one person in a peer group flaunts their tab or a personal mobile, it has a ripple effect, and the entire group hankers for the same. You must very strongly resist this 'itch'.

Here is the other side of the coin, when your peer group has friends, who are good in academics, they motivate you to make efforts to match their performance. When your peers achieve their targets, it should work as a wake-up call for you, or else you will lag. Taking inspiration from them will bring a positive change in your way of working.

Peers can themselves pressure each other in rectifying things or doing the right things in the first place. When you are with your peers, you watch them keenly, you can pick up some good habits from them, like being on time, using less screen time, etc. The highest contribution of a peer group can be your overall changed perception towards life from negative to positive and turn pressure into motivation. It can become a positive force that will push you in the right direction. For this, you have to be on your toes and listen to the warning 'whistles' whenever you tend to stray into the wrong paths.

Before I move forward, I wish to mention here the peer pressure that parents feel. They should not only be well aware of it but resist it too. Father may have peers among his school/college friends or business acquaintances; similarly, mother in her kitty or among friends and relatives. They not only feel the pressure, but they also create it by comparing their son/daughter with that of their peers. They feel a lot of stress and pass it on to their child to score better than the children of their peer group. Most parents always compare their kids with others without realising that they are different. A fish cannot win a tree climbing competition when pitted against a monkey. Let it excel at swimming.

Parents should be mindful of their kid's age before bringing them any expensive gadget or allowing them outings at odd hours and not do it under pressure from their peers.

Kids, as they grow, are usually with their peer company more than the time they spend under adult supervision. Kids do get bullied in school for several reasons, and we cannot stop this from happening every time. We can teach the bullied child to learn from his experience and thus to act better with other kids. They understand that it is incorrect to bully others. They already know how bad it feels with their own experience.

The pressure exists among all ages, just that it is the maximum during adolescence. Peers play a prime part in the lives of these young adults and influence their behaviour to quite an extent. It is known as the hallmark of adolescent experience!

Going down memory lane, I tried to think hard if I went through this peer pressure when I was at this stage. I also asked myself if I had any parental pressure too in those years. Well, I'm sure no one better than my mum can bring these answers to me; she is the most reliable source to know about me, I bet!

The reason why I am going back to my old days is only to understand the situations and handle them appropriately now. I have been advising my kids from time to time in their day-to-day life for several things. Though they do certain activities regularly which are already known to them, a reminder is still needed. For example, brushing teeth at night, setting time-table, changing into night wears, drinking water, and so on. These everyday sets of instructions or reminders are often enough to see their long-long faces. From time to time, I also remind them about not getting carried away by their peers. I feel a regular reminder is needed to counter the peer pressure.

Today was a different drama altogether. She behaved weird, irritated for nothing, and cranky too. After confirming that neither there had been a fight with anyone nor was she hungry, the matter was hard to understand; until she came and asked me for it. What was it? Wait, I'm coming to the point, but let me clarify who came to me this time. Okay, so this one is about my younger one, Anya (age: 12 years); we can call her pre-teen or tween, who was studying in the sixth standard then.

Getting back to the long face drama, the issue of the day was a grave one. It was about her not having a phone when all her friends had it.

"All my friends have it, and I also need it!" she proclaimed.

Anyways, we can always cut short 'all' from the comment above as that stands in common for everything for which they seek permission. We have heard of similar things many times, be it visiting a friend's place or watching a particular movie. Well, peer pressure is a critical issue of all ages. Earlier it used to be like, who has a fast-moving car or a better doll. From having a TV video game to having an X-Box was a big deal. Well, now it is about who has a better phone?

She did not request but demanded a personal phone as if it was her birth-right to have one. Her arguments were strong as to why she must have a phone. She was full prepared with solid reasoning, so was I. I stated with equally strong reasonings that she was still not at the correct age; and cannot get a phone. I clarified to her that I had no plans of giving her a mobile phone until she was at least fourteen years old. The reason being I was already suffering after making a similar mistake with my elder one, Tiara. Let me clear this; it wasn't me who made this blunder. As usual, her father went against me and had gifted her a phone on her 12th birthday. The argument got a little heated up after about 20 minutes. I included all the points from my childhood referring to our life which was so lively without phones, and how we used to have a super fun time without them. I did not forget to mention that the landlines (telephones) were allowed after we reached class seven. That too was under supervision, and we could make only a limited number of calls. We were made sure to pay attention in school classes because we had no other source of cross-checking our homework or class works.

After a long argument, it turned to be one-sided because I went on and on. I felt that Anya was in deep thought, not knowing what to say at the end. She had an expression of sigh after losing the argument and was probably long lost into something. I very well knew that her demand for the cell phone was no more about its features or about playing games; those things were available on my phone too. At this age, they demand to fit in the group to which they belong. Similarly, her need was essentially to be at par with the other friends of her existing group, her peers. It is one of the examples where the pressure cooker of life is evident – the peer pressure!

I wondered that it wasn't a small thing to deal with for Anya. Thus I needed a solution so that she does not feel anyway less than her friends with phones. I went back deep into thoughts, thinking about my time when I had felt some pressure of a similar kind. Though we did not have phones in those times yet, there were many other things to crave. It depended on your interest totally, whether it was about the latest game, a toy, a book, or a doll (it was a great feeling to own a Barbie doll). As we grew up, it changed to going out with friends to either for lunch, a recreational park, or a movie. The movie was the last thing to be allowed, and it needed quite a bit of convincing capacity. I was allowed to go only because the rest of the parents had allowed my friends the movie outing. These mini restrictions, or call them certain principles which my parents followed, taught me to accept 'No'. Along with it came the acceptance that it is okay not to get what you ask for; this is how my parents dealt with me. They made sure that despite these peer pressures, their daughter would be fine.

I got my answer, and I decided to be firm with Anya and encourage her by explaining the positive side of not having a phone. In other words, I would teach her how to save herself from not being cooked under peer pressure.

There was another thought that was constantly running in my mind that made me question myself. If I was lenient with many things, only to cope with the pressure around me as a parent. It is not just that my daughters are under peer pressure, but I was too under some parental peer pressure. Was I allowing Tiara too much leeway as per her age only because I wanted to make up for other things that I failed to do for her? I realised that it is not just her but me too who has pressure as a parent.

I then understood that it is vital to keep a check on myself. I must make sure that the things that make me say 'yes' don't happen due to the peer pressure I face, for which otherwise I would have said 'no'. Well, today it's about getting a phone under peer pressure; tomorrow might ask to date someone or try alcohol, who knows? Everything has a correct time.

I have mentioned another incident my elder daughter experienced, but rather share it from the horse's mouth under the Teenager section of this chapter. This incident reaffirmed my belief that a subtle reminder here; and a nudge there helps these kids to find the right path. It helps them discern the right from the wrong. Don't overdo, do not pester them; they are more intelligent than we were at their age. But don't get frustrated when they don't listen and argue. Do not stop telling them about the negative peer pressure! So over to you kids...!

The Pressure Cooker of Life (teens)

Anya's view

(at age 10)

I don't know why my mom is unwilling to give me a phone while all my friends have it. She has convinced dad now to agree to the same. Had it been in class five, I would have understood that I was younger, but even Tiara didi got her phone when she was in class six, then why not me? Since they have allowed me to go out with my friends, they must understand that it is required to call the driver and other people to coordinate my drop and pick up. It is essential as I need it for necessary communications. Leave the rest, mom-dad should understand that at this age all my friends have one and I need it too! Even if not my private phone, they can allow me to carry one of the extra handsets we have at home or dad's other number that he uses; anything would do.

It is so bugging to ask others for a phone whenever I need to make a phone call. No matter how much I explain this genuine reason for having a phone, mum never understands. What do I do if Mum did not get a phone until she grew up; Well, is it my problem? I do not want to wait till I grow up to that age. Anyways, she says that the phone never existed when she was in school, so how would she ever need it at all. She wasn't even allowed to go out with friends frequently; it was mostly on their birthdays when the kids were permitted an outing, that too after class 8. For sure, either she did not have many friends at that time, or she makes up stories to convince me. God help me! I only need a phone, a simple phone. I did not even demand an iPhone; a simple smartphone would do, be it any!

My phone arguments were going to be often, I guess. It is because it is high time that they understand my need for it. I recently fell into another debate with mom when she did not allow me to go out for a movie. All my friends were permitted. I don't know why every time does mum has to ask so many questions. She says she was not allowed frequent outings like we do and especially for movies. After a long argument and debate, I felt angry but could not react much as I knew it would drive me to another punishment. I spoke in a high pitch, trying to cope up with my rage. I wanted to punch on somebody and knock the person down. I went to my room and pushed away my badminton racket on the floor that obstructed me on my way. I threw the stationary lying on the bed and made space to sit, and took deep breaths. I closed my eyes and started to count 1 to 10 slowly. I calmed myself down and felt better. I told myself that it was pointless trying to convince her as she would never understand the pain of FOMO (Fear of missing out)! She never understood that not having a phone gave me an outcast feeling, so she never will understand the feeling of being left out. It feels like being friendless. I would be sitting here alone while all my friends would be together watching the movie with popcorn and nachos. She does not bother about my emotions at all. Never did she ever understand anything about me.

Tiara's story:

I was studying in the ninth standard and had an outing program with a school friend Naina. Mom allowed without much fuss with a parting warning to be alert, take care, and return in time. We went to a very famous roadside fast-food centre. Varun, from the boys' school, a friend of Naina, also joined us there. We placed our order and stood there waiting on the side path for it. Varun pulled out a few cigarettes from his pack of squares and asked for a matchbox from the shopkeeper.

I was surprised but not much until he lighted two sticks and offered one to Naina. Then came the shock when see her accepted it eagerly and put it to her lips as if she had been waiting for it. Next was my turn. Varun offered one to me; at that moment, a series of thoughts flashed in my mind. The first one was my image with a cigarette loosely dangling from my lips, and I was blowing off smoke circles. Thankfully it was just a flash. I had almost extended my hand to accept the stick but then rang in my ears mom's parting word: "Be alert!" I also remembered the videos shown in school that warned against the ill effect of falling into the pit of tobacco and other addictions.

"Omg! It is exactly the moment when I have to say NO", I reminded myself. I knew that this was 'the' moment when one could get carried away into tobacco addiction. Another feeling which took over me was, "What if mom and dad come to know?" I was scared to think that if mom questions about smoking, I would have no answer.

I had never seen children of my age fag, and hence, it was clear that this isn't for me. This realisation, along with an array of thoughts, happened within a few seconds! While Varun still waited for me to accept the cigarette which he had extended towards me. I said, "No! no, I have never tried it; I do not smoke!" I was still pushed by both of them as they said, "It is alright dude...everyone fags; it is no big deal. Be cool, give it a try, don't be a sissy!" I so precisely understood what mom meant when she talked about 'wrong peer pressure.'

I was happy as I did not succumb to the temptation to try something new, a dare, or negative peer pressure.

Though I write calmly now, I was then clueless about how to react. I was speechless and was still wondering at the audacity of my friends. I was fearful and numb. On hearing the incident, mom went speechless. With her tear-filled eyes, she thanked God and gave me a tight hug. We both were a mixed bag of emotions. Happy, grateful, and a bit fearful too with the thought: "What if!?" I was so thankful for not getting carried away. I was thanking God and my parents for it working outright. At the same time, I felt sad for my friends who probably were already a victim of peer pressure.

CHAPTER 11

NUTRITIONIST MOM

"You must eat veggies and soup today."

"I don't like such boring food, Mom!"

"It is both healthy and tasty. You need to eat and decide,"

"Can I order pasta?"

"No, not again. You had pizza yesterday."

"I won't eat this healthy food as well."

...

This argument can burn calories way too much than expected because it takes a lot of effort each day. I don't know the logic of teaching chapters on Food & Nutrition, and why at all are the kids taught about a balanced diet and junk food? Alas! Food has become nothing but a common point of argument that happens almost every day. It does not matter who, among the two, I argued with because the other one automatically gets the advantage.

Meals are supposed to be eaten in a happy mood so that we benefit from them far more than their nutritional value. But when you have another argument over the meal and get to see the same sulking face of your kids, what do you choose to do? It seems there is always one meal at least that starts with an argument every single day. It is either of them or maybe me who begins the meal-squabble. They always team up to fight against me when it comes to food. I fail to understand how they expect me to allow 'junkies' like pizza pasta to satisfy their hunger. I definitely cannot let it be a frequent substitute for healthy food like veggies and soup?

As usual, with my thinking cap on, I went back to my teenage days to recollect how much patience my Mom' had with me when it came to food. I have to accept that I was a picky eater, not only because I was choosy and moody. In those days, the argument was like, "You will have to eat whatever food is prepared, without wasting a bite on the plate." We could take more helping, in case we wanted to. If not, we had to finish the portions served on the plate at least. Next time we knew we had to take less and ask for more if need be. There was no option of wasting or skipping food; lunch and dinners were mandatory. Fancy food items were to be eaten only at some other hour. It was the rule of the house, and it needed to be followed by hook or by crook.

I also remember my Mom' agreeing to allow Maggi, fries, pizza, and pasta but not frequently. We did not have it as regularly as our kids eat today. We were also allowed to go out to buy rice puffs or 'Muri' and Puchkas from the vendor across the street, but never did these things substitute our main meal. However, with the kids today, sometimes the dish is an issue or the preparation or the taste is a problem. Quite often, Swiggy and Zomato delivery boys are spotted ringing our doorbell.

One day, I did not give up and equally confronted Tiara about her reason for not eating food happily. She murmured in a feeble voice, with her head down, but I heard what she said, "Who likes to get fat" so I asked how she justifies eating junkies, which will make her even fatter. As usual, I advised her that the healthy portion on her plate would rather keep her healthy and not make her fat. To which came Anya's impromptu reply, "We would rather eat less of what we like to eat rather than finishing this entire plate of home-cooked meal". Okay, so she applied her logic. "I agree," said Tiara, and then I had to finally surrender as it was better to lose a small battle than to lead to war.

Food denials had become part of their life. Tiara started to realise a bit only after she experienced blackouts due to low haemoglobin levels, and she became lazy due to low energy.

I suggested to them that we better sit with their biology book and re-read the food pyramid. Anya gave me a look as if she was telling herself that 'Oh God, mum is too much." I had already surrendered the battle by allowing them to order their favourite food. Hopefully, now they would pay attention when I explain the chapter that states nutrients and their qualities. Anya had no option as I insisted upon her to bring her biology book. While we read the side effects of eating frequent junk food in the chapter, Tiara smiled within making sure it does not show up on her lips. She was unaware that it reflected in her eyes. This secret smile of hers told me that she was indeed aware of the value of nutritious food but needed a concrete reminder. She gathered all her patience and said, "Okay, mom. I know what you are saying is correct. Junk food cannot replace veggies". Anya knew that I had cornered her. She smartly accepted her mistake and asked me about what to do next.

Since they were cooperating enough, it was back on me to take out a win-win solution that would work the best for us both. Then we began a healthy discussion about food and diet. We mutually decided upon certain days of having junk food, but on the other days would be home-cooked food without a fuss ('without any fuss' was the highlight). Thus, the mantra of healthy living was finalised that said nutritious food on most number of days and few days of indulging in the junk. I even tried to incorporate the habit of eating food without watching TV. I just gave it a try hoping they would accept this as well, but no, it did not work at all. Do not expect them to understand everything at a go!

Understanding and agreeing to eat more healthy food was already an incredible achievement. We were all happy with the idea. These teens are sometimes unpredictable; they can surprise you with their decisions. The war ended peacefully without leading to a battle. Happy me!

Nutrition by teens

I must say that mom never compelled me to have soups, salads, and juices. It would be a white lie to say that my mom is always after my life to have healthy food.

Thanks to the food pyramid, I had it set inside my head, but I did that only to fetch marks in the biology paper. I did not intend to choose healthy leafy things over mayonnaise. Having home-cooked meals have become a frightening task for me, as I know that the food will also cause an argument with mom! Of course, clashes are not healthy, so could someone please tell her that the meal then becomes unhealthy too.

On the other hand, if she could ever understand my point. I tried to explain to her that my pizzas are healthy. The base is of whole wheat bread. It has lots of veggies like tomatoes, onion, mushrooms, bell peppers used as toppings, and some cheese for sure. Aren't these healthy veggies? I usually dab the extra oil with a tissue and make sure I consume as much as needed; similarly, my burgers are also healthy. I mostly eat a homemade one, except for McDonalds on rare occasions. The buns are whole wheat bread, and the patties are home-cooked topped with lettuce, cheese, and mayo which are supposed to be healthy. I agree that the cola –float or the can of coke or red bull can be harmful, but how is a burger or a pizza not good? It is just a way to have your meal differently with similar ingredients, that's all. But forget it explaining this to mom would be like draining out your energy.

It has become an everyday matter. Every meal after meal, my mom starts the same topic about having good food, nutritious food, omg! Finally, she confronted me and asked about my regular eating habits. She tried to make me realise that I do not have a healthy diet in my daily food. She went on as usual. Suddenly a brilliant answer popped up in my mind; I told her that I would rather eat less of what I like than more of what I don't like. I was impressed by my dialogue.

Mom did not give up anyways; she just nodded as if thinking of my defeat with some other attack. I got the shock of my life when mom came up with the undefeatable idea of the day. Her attack wasn't verbal; it came veiled in the form of a Biology Chapter. She made us read the chapter on Food and Nutrition. I could not deny it as I also had a bio exam the next day.

After visiting the food pyramid, and re-reading all the ill effects of junk food, the benefits of nutritional food, now was the time to make some worthy decisions. The chapter was quite convincing in favour of home food, but our taste buds were revolting. Though unwillingly, we had to accept few facts that homemade food had to be eaten without fuss, whereas we could indulge in junk only on a few days. Oh God! is it possible to interchange the days? Because I only know how I crave to eat more what I am allowed to eat less.

There was no option, and thus we had to settle with the decision accepting it with smiles on our faces. At least something is better than nothing. Anyways, I know rules are meant to be broken, and I hope these off days too will fall apart in some time. I cannot imagine my life with a plate full of healthy food in hand and that too without TV.

I had thought we had difficult days ahead but was proved wrong as mum prepared for us 'healthy junk food' at home for us. Yes, you read it right! She made us whole wheat pasta; we had delicious pizza with the toppings of our choice – corn, olives, tomato, onion, bell pepper, and loads of cheese. She also baked the pizza base at home. We were served yummy dishes from various cuisines, like Risotto, Thai green curry & rice, Hakka noodles with Chilly potatoes, Aglio olio, Mexican Rice, Vada Pav and so many more. They were all delicious and yummy. I'm sure mum pampered us out of the way such that we do not crave to order junkies. 'Nutritious junk food'- was not served to us every day. We also had to eat regular meals like rice, dal, chapatti, and green veggies.

But again, however healthy and tasty home-cooked food variety is, nothing can beat the Dominos pizzas, Subway sandwiches, McDonald's' burgers, Yautcha's sushi and deserts, Fenicia's Dimsums, Chinese at Bar-B-que, and not to forget the food at The Grid, PaPaYa, One8.commune and SAZ ! In short, life cannot run without outside food. Thus, it is better to keep a balance. So, guys once in a while, why not give moms rest and let our Swiggy and Zomato friends work?! (read a grin:D)

CHAPTER -12

BULLYING

Stooping shoulders, downside curvy lips, draggy feet with the school bag trailing behind. Is this a familiar scene for you too? Though not every day, yet this is how my little one comes back from school once in a while. This scene became frequent with an added grumpy hello in response to my lively greeting. I observed it for a few days but then had to tell her to drop this indifferent kind of an attitude no matter how tired she was. It did not work, and she continued in the same way. I finally confronted her by asking what the problem was.

I was all set to charge her of how discourteous she was behaving lately. I was all prepared to get hold of her the next time when she replied sullenly. Like any other day, Anya returned from school with her everyday demeanour, no smile! Though I was all prepared to pin her with my dialogues, but one look at her told my motherly instinct that something was not right. I hugged her without giving a second thought. She paused but then hugged me back equally tight. This exchange was enough for me to know that something was worrying her. It was also for her assurance that I am there. With no exchange of words, she sat down on the couch. I held her hand and asked, "Trust all is well" Tears that stood in her eyes now rolled down her cheeks. She had held them back for long, but it was time for them to flow and give her relief. I allowed her to have her own time. The matter seemed much severe than her long face conveyed.

It wasn't an easy task to dig out things from her. After around fifteen minutes of questioning and guessing, I finally succeeded in opening her up. She told me that she parted from her group friends due to the shuffling rule. They were all in the same section, but she was missing them due to her new place in the classroom. Oh! The problem was not grave, I thought. I suggested her become friendly with the girls she was sharing the bench with; so that she feels equally good with this new set of friends. Her old buddies would always be there, and now she would have more friends to call her own. This suggestion did not seem to be convincing her much, and she came up with the real story. Anya was uncomfortable and felt out of place amongst the kids with whom she was sitting. She confessed that she felt left out, as people in the new group considered themselves superior. She wasn't able to cope with them. She went on to describe how she felt aloof and left out. I gave her my listening ears, but this time I did not interrupt. I kept quiet as I wanted her to share everything, what was going on in her mind. I could understand that she was genuinely feeling rejected. For a girl of eleven years, it is quite a big deal.

The topic did not end here. As Anya moved further into details, I figured out that it included bullying as well. I was worried upon knowing about the so-called 'the bosses group' that ordered the classmates to perform unacceptable tasks. After getting to know about how she and few more students were teased and bullied by this group, I asked her to jot down all the things they were said to perform. I looked at the list in surprise that read like this:

- *Pick your bag on your head and take a round of the class*
- *Pull your best friend's cheeks till they turn red*
- *Spill water such that someone's uniform gets wet*
- *Buy them noodles from the canteen during recess.*
- *Wipe the dirty desk with your handkerchief*
- *Handover your lunch box to them*

My heart broke on reading this list, and I got to know the spoilt bunch of the newly turned middle schoolers. I did not show her that I felt bad for her. Instead, I wiped her tears and told her that these people were merely challenges for her. And that she is both sensible and capable of dealing with them. She calmed down with my assurance that we would work this out together if need be. Then followed my own school experience of having that left-out kind of a feeling, I narrated to her a few incidents. She smiled and gradually laughed hearing my stories, some were facts, and some, I instantly made up to see her laugh. I then explained that the instances I had faced in school then. They affected me so much in those days but do not matter today. And then we both sat to strategize few other things about her next day at school. We made a mutual plan on which she had to act the following day. She was overjoyed, and so was I. We giggled about a few of her happenings in the school, then ended on a laughing note.

Tiara returned home after attending the extra class in her school. On knowing the matter, she got furious and wanted to teach the Bosses group a lesson. She was concerned about her little sister getting bullied by her classmates. Anya, who was happy to see her sister stand for her, hugged Tiara and said, "Thank you! Di, but Mum has a plan. I'm sure things will work out that way. I will extend my hand of friendship and keep all my patience to accept their rude replies if any. All I need to do is stay strong & not get affected by them. I need not do any task under pressure. Also, I have to happily ignore their nasty comments on me once I deny doing their assigned tasks. It is as simple as that." And I added, "If this plan does not work, then we always have the option open to report the matter to the school authorities if serious."

Both me and Tiara were proud of her, and we gave her a tight hug together. I saw her relaxed. She understood that these kinds of incidents are irrelevant for life. She was able to bring some power back and regained her confidence.

She was much better by the evening. My little warrior was all set to fight her own battle with complete confidence. We both slept peacefully that night, and she looked forward to another day at school.

Bullying –sufferings by teens

I returned from school and entered the home, tried my best to keep a smile on my face. Thoughts of the torment meted out to me by my new bossy classmates today, who had forced me to throw water on another friend prevented it. I was dragging my bag and did look at my mom as she opened the door. I waited for her usual reprimand, but after getting a brief stare from her, there came a tight hug as a surprise. Her loving touch melted all the frustration I had because of the classroom harassment, and tears stood in my eyes.

I understood that mom has somehow smelled my discomfort and would insist on knowing the details. A thousand thoughts were running in my mind, do I snitch on my classmates? Would it not be against 'friend code? Do I tell her partly? She cannot help in these matters! While hugging me, she gently whispered in my ear, "What's the matter; what is eating you?" Well, I knew I would hold back anything from her. I tried to fend her for some time, but soon with tears rolling down my cheeks, I narrated today's incident. Also, how due to the shuffling rule, my friends and me It separated. Mom has shared my bossy friends' story in some detail, so I don't feel like writing it again.

But here is what I have been going through for some time, which culminated as a mental burden. It distracted me from my studies.

Here is my story:

Have you heard of Monday blues? Yes, that sad feeling that keeps you unwilling to go to school. I had these blues not only on Mondays but all the days of the week. What gave me these blues was none other than my classmates, especially those Monday mornings that had exams. It was indeed tough to have a sound sleep on a Sunday night because the next day was a working day after a break of two days.

It was a similar Monday morning, and I got nightmares that my friends were trying to drag me out from the bed, only to pull my leg. Oh gosh! I woke up with a startle. But then I realised that I was sleeping, and it was time to get ready for school. I sat still and took a few minutes to get out of bed. I knew it would take me 5 minutes to get ready and another 5 to get and pack my bag. Thinking of having that glass full of uninteresting banana shake added to my woes. The only pleasant time was the thirty minutes' drive to school when we both listen to RJ Praveen at 93.5 Red FM. He plays the latest numbers, and that makes the car drive interesting.

The only thing that worried me was the Chemistry exam that I was supposed to face soon after the assembly. The equations are a rigid deal. I don't know why we have to learn to balance them; learning their valency, atomicity, etc., is such a waste of time, I tell you. I have never seen my mom or my dad do it ever in their life. We have such an illogical system of education, huh! The main point is that my life isn't a bed of roses; whether it is about studies or friends, nothing stands in place at the moment. Well! I am not a bad student, do not get me wrong at this, because I have been doing quite well in all the other subjects. Chemistry is not my cup of tea. Days get easier when other things in the school go right, but no, I was having a tough time in school, and I hated entering my class. This situation wasn't the same earlier. I have always had good friends and many friends. We have always had fun during recess and even during classes. I don't know what went wrong with this sixth standard.

You already know that everything started when our teacher shuffled our places. All the students got rearranged, and mostly some spoiled kids got into my section. They were loud, naughty, weird, and unapologetic, unlike the previous lot. The only thing they were good at was sports, in which I had no interest. So, we had just nothing in common to mingle. Thus, I felt like an alien in the class who was unable to communicate at all. People stopped even glancing at me in the assembly line because I started keeping quiet and reserved. Finally, I stopped talking to anyone and found comfort within my shell. I had a conception that I was becoming quite a bore.

No one wanted to have me in their team, be it sports or a project. People called me an idiot, which shattered me to the core. All of this gradually brought down my academic performance. Other kids used to talk about their outings with friends and how much fun they had at the weekend; their conversation was louder than needed, as if it was to make me feel sh*t*y and left out. People ignored me way too much. These smart ones or, I can say over–smart ones bullied us by ordering us to perform annoying tasks. It is why I lost absolute interest in school.

Mom was compassionate towards me on hearing my suffering. She gave me a simple yet magical solution to my problems. Mom was very logical, and her assurance of things getting better gave me a sigh of relief. Very sweetly, she told me her own stories of getting bullied in school. Most surprisingly, some of her stories seemed like that of my own; things truly happened a similar way in my case. Her stories were funny as well as message-giving. Tiara di was ready to help me too; she has always been my best friend. Mum did not finish there. She made me jot down a few needed cures to my problems that could help me handle them with ease. I am sharing the same with you.

1. Let Go - The first and foremost thing to do is ignore the people who try to act over smart or are popular because of their mischief. Remember that these people behave so because they seek attention and are insecure about their own life and friends. They probably do not have people to share their stories with; do not get affected by such kids, and let go.

2. Believe in yourself - It is equally important to concentrate only on your strengths. When you pay attention to your abilities and strengths, then only you can build a positive self-image. In turn, this will help you tackle the situations boldly without getting affected by the wrongdoings of others.

3. Adult guidance – Share your problems with an adult. It can be your parents, counsellor at school, an elder brother, or a sister who is much senior to you. Sharing your problems with them will always bring the best of suggestions. They have gone through such situations and know better ways to handle them.

4. Be friendly – Try and be friends with at least anyone from the so-called 'popular group.' During difficult times it gets easier to balance situations and prevent them from going from bad to worse.

5. Be your boss – Never follow the mass, rather be the trendsetter. It will help you stay happy with your own set of rules for yourself.

I was joyous to have shared my problems with mum. I was wrong that she would not be able to help me. I woke up happy and fresh the next day and was all set to face the group in class.

CHAPTER –13

REPORT CARDS

"Success is never final and failure not fatal" – by Winston Churchill

This is a famous saying...

I was tired, exhausted, and simply drained out. Not so much physically, but pretty much mentally. I was emotionally depleted on seeing my daughter stressed and heartbroken about her annual results. It is easy to take care of them when they fall down and get physically hurt, but the bruise they get emotionally is a burdensome task to deal with.

It was the day of the results of the final term, though I had a pep talk with her in the morning, yet she went to school nervous and anxious. Me telling her that I was so very proud of her as she had prepared for the exam all by herself did not really work. She smiled at me when I said, " I would be satisfied with whatever your results shall be because I know that you have worked hard for it without any guidance."

She went to the school with a brave attitude even after knowing that she wouldn't fetch good marks in Mathematics. She also hoped for some miracle to happen which could bring her aggregate above 80%. Though I assured her but felt some anxiety myself. Throughout the afternoon, I was concerned, not for her low marks but for having low self-esteem. She entered home with a smile, though the twinkle in her eyes was missing. I expected her to reveal her low marks in Maths but for sure an aggregate of 80%. She looked at me and told me the unexpected. I was happy to see that her pass with flying colours. But my heart sank to hear that she was still unhappy. The reason being she did not score 90% in 'all' her subjects; her focus was only on the ones where she did not score 90%. Although she had performed brilliantly well in all of them along with Maths (which she wasn't expecting), she still remained unhappy. Her focus seemed to be only on the subjects in which she attained less than 90.

Suddenly she hugged me and said, "Mom, I feel broken and bad." I hugged her back. Tears rolled down her cheeks to flood the pillow. Her pain was not only about the low marks, but she was also expecting to do better than her competing mates in the class. Her friends had got the 'excellence card' for their performance above 90% in all subjects. She was feeling ashamed because she knew she was capable of getting it too. She was hating the feeling that some other classmate had taken the position she had been holding for the last 2 years.

I let her tears flow and gave space to her emotions. I heard her out so that she would feel better and peaceful. Once her tears dried, I smiled at her and hugged her again. This was not the time for my lecture, so I waited for her to speak up more if she wanted to add anything else. She was silent, so I told her that I very well knew she wouldn't get even 80% in maths since she had not practiced it well, and it was fair enough because maths needed consistency. She did not sit with maths work despite telling her several times. She also got irritated with my reminders. I said, "Your classmates got what they deserved; the excellence card is not for you this time, which is alright. One gets what one deserves, so do not give up. Do not get disheartened and keep working hard."

She then agreed and said, "I know maths cannot be done overnight and needs constant practice. She told me what I intended to say, that next time, she would practice it chapter-wise parallelly with the school.

I was happy that I did not have to lecture her about this, and she realised it all by herself. The only message that I conveyed to her was that "success is not guaranteed, and failure is never final." She smartly took out her diary and write down in bold letters "PRACTICE MATHS EVERY DAY"!

"Failure is a failure no matter how you fail" – says the teen.

It was a dreadful night. My eyes wide open were gazing at the ceiling. Was I trying to figure out the architecture of the room? Definitely not!

I was tensed and stressed about my annual results the next day. No matter how hard I tried to sleep but my eyes would open up at the sound of the ticking wall clock. It seemed that the clock had suddenly become loud and slow. Did it need batteries to keep moving, or was it me who needed to stop staring at it? After hours of tossing, I don't know when I fell asleep.

Fear of not earning a merit card could be a silly reason for not getting proper sleep. Could it take away your night's sleep? How stupid of me! Mum had given me a long hug and had assured me that she was proud of me irrespective of my performance. Moreover, because I did not seek her help at all for my exams. She probably had more expectations, but she used encouraging words only to console me. If I could at all read her mind, it would say: "I wish she got the 'excellence card' It was not wrong of her to expect that. I was consistently getting it for the last two years.

It was morning school assembly when the teacher announced the names of those students who received the 'excellence card' this year. I do not want to blow my own trumpet, but the fact remains that I have been an 'excellence cardholder' past two consecutive years. My friends kept asking me if I would make it a hat-trick. They wanted to know my level of excitement. This is a familiar scenario and happens every year. I always answer them with an ear-to-ear grin. This time it was different because I smiled only to change the topic. I knew I would not win the excellence card this time, but I tried not to display the same on my face.

My palms were cold, and my mouth was as dry as a desert. My throat had a lump, and my forehead was sweaty. Anxiety and panic were all over me; I'm sure there were many like me in the assembly who shivered due to their own reasons for being anxious.

Then the names began one by one. It was the middle school assembly, so class six stood first on the list. The most dreaded time had to be faced. The names came one by one starting with section A.

From Class 6A, we have Ananya Gupta; please give her a big round of applause!

From Class 6B, we have Seema Sureka; please give her a big hand,

Coming up next is (this was my class, and I wanted to shut my ears so desperately) Anisha Swami from Class 6C; please give her a big hand! Though I was fully prepared not to hear my name, yet something went wrong with me. I felt a short circuit in my brain, and I stood numb. I was lost in my own world, and my ears stopped working. I could no more hear any sound around me. I faintly clapped my hands, which were in motion ever since the names were being called out, but my brain was in a snooze mode.

My mind went into calculative mode. There were very few kids in the entire class 6 who had received excellence cards, which means only a few of them could achieve 90% or above in all subjects. Was that not really sad for the school as well, I thought. It was tragic for me when my name wasn't called out amongst them, and the tiny little hope of miracle died. I don't really know why it hit me so hard when I had already surrendered to the fact that I would not get it. Why did I find myself demolished when I did not get the privilege to walk up the stage? Why did I get disheartened for not getting the smile from my principal and a pat on my back? Why? I asked myself several times but did not get a perfect answer.

There was a probability that I had always got an excellence card, so I was feeling terrible this time. Maybe very few people in the school received it, or it may be because I had not written my answers well to have received a 90 in all subjects. After all, it was my first experience of giving an 80 marks paper. I was maybe under my own pressure of excelling in the Subjects and getting flying colours. Somehow my mind bounced by anxiety & make my performance fall below expectations, or I might have been overconfident. No matter what it was, I was feeling ridiculous for something I already knew about.

I went home wearing a smile on my face, but my eyes were still lost. My heart cried, "Mom, it hurts!" although I could not speak it out. My mom is a gadget to sense all my inner emotions, so I never have an escape. One look at me, and she understood that there was much more behind my smile. Her hugs are eternal bliss. Despite all the things that I go against, I accept mom's hugs have always been the best source of my strength. She makes my confidence flow back in me. I kept a brave face until the tight hug came and let open the tank of my tears. Thankfully, I did not receive any lecture at that moment, which usually automatically comes from her when I do something wrong.

I instantly promised myself that I would practice maths regularly as a mum too had suggested. I made a pact of being attentive in the class and not keeping things due for my tuition teacher to explain later. I did not reveal this to mum but wish to prove it to her by my actions. She always says action speaks louder than words. Maybe my overconfidence had pulled me down. It is always good to be confident and which can come only when I remind myself from time to time about regular studies and practices.

I had not taken mom's words seriously that class 6 would be very different from class 5. She had told me that it would be a jump in the syllabus, and I will not cope without being regular in my studies. As usual, I was proved wrong. Class 6 wasn't a piece of cake. It was one of the milestones in the Academics hierarchy.

I needed to forgive myself for my own mistakes. I needed to forget what had happened and come out of the pity feeling I was developing for myself. Mum always says that self–realisation is a big thing. Once we realise where we have gone wrong, it does not take much to correct and move forward. I knew that I need to make proper rules for myself and follow them diligently. Forgiving myself and mending my ways will bring my power back, and then I will re-start with a bang. It was now time to try, try and try till I succeeded. Mom always quotes Winston Churchill "Success is never final and Failure not fatal.

Finally, my sad mood evaporated in thin air, and I was back to my cheerful self once again. Watch out! grade-7 as I come all set and prepared to knock you down with flying colours.

So, guys, is it not weird that we focus on what we do not have and ignore what we hold. I was crestfallen for not scoring 90% in all subjects; whereas, I should have rejoiced on attaining much better than average in all Subjects. I did not get an excellence card, but I was still in the top 10 students in the entire class VI!! We need to be grateful for what we achieve and strive for better instead of ruing for what we could not accomplish. I might have focused on half-empty glass, but I am now hell-bent on filling it up! Guys, focus on the roses, not on thorns...consider this: It's no roses that have thorns, but it's thorns that have roses

CHAPTER -14

VALUE OF MONEY

"Mom," said Tiara with a beaming face. "Remember it is 1ˢᵗ October, and I badly need my pocket money and my birthday allowance when I return from school". I have no money left to give a big treat to my friends! Do remember, you folks had promised me last year to increase my pocket money this year."

"Yeah, sure, dear!" I replied and added, "We shall discuss it when you come back."

"What is there to discuss?" There came a frown on her face. Though I felt a crooked smile fleetingly come and go. Maybe I imagined things.

She was all set to leave for school and had a class test, so I did not wish to irritate her. Placated her by saying that it was just the increase in the amount that we needed to discuss.

She left but left me with some food for thought. We had a big argument last year around this time. She was adamant about an increase in her pocket money. It ended when we assured her that we would consider it next year and had put forth some conditions. We take care of all her expenses. She does not have to spend on gifts she gets on birthdays for the family members or our anniversary or her birthday. She also does not use her pocket money to pay for her lunches, or ice cream, etc. Once in a while, she does use it for giving a treat to her friends at school. Here too, at times, she cajoles to her dad to part some money for it. She also received money from relatives during festivals like Rakhi, Diwali, etc. I know it very well that she does not squander money. So, where is she spending it? Why does she need pocket money so desperately? Why does she need an increase in this allowance? Last year on this day only we had discussed the value of money and how we should inculcate the habit of saving it. It seems all the previous year's deliberation about money's worth had gone down the drain. I was at a loss how to drill the significance of money and its value in her mind. The idea behind starting her pocket money was only to teach her to value money. I felt this was the most effective way to train her to keep an account of her spending. I had also introduced to her the idea of keeping aside some money for charity.

I went back to my growing up days when shopping used to be a necessity and not a luxury. For us, an amount of twenty rupees meant it was party time for muri, puchkas, and toffees. More so, in those days, money had to be earned by playfully doing small tasks at home. In a way, these were lessons that taught us money was hard-earned. When I was around seven-eight years old, I did fun activities like polished our father's shoes. I kept them ready before he left for office. Then happily gave him a salute after he handed over few coins in our hands. We took them with pride and looked forward to more such activities. I have another example to mention when coins that fell out from papa's pockets while lying down on the bed belonged to the person who claimed them first and collected them in the palm. "Yayy...!" was the feeling to own those few coins. Shopping used to be occasional, especially on birthdays, festivals, and other special events. We learned to spend as well as do our savings and charity from our allowance. Money wasn't readily available to us. Times have changed for sure, and we cannot compare today. When I look back, I wonder how my mom had control over us and had strict rules. Tantrums were unacceptable under any circumstance. We did not know what tantrums were. We learned to value money by simple methods and means.

I thought of sitting with Tiara and discuss her needs, point by point. The motive was to explain the value of saving money. There was no use telling my childhood story because I was sure to get a retort, "Mom, please stop 'in my time' stories; they are history, not valid today!"

Also, discussions don't work in the form of a lecture. They know what to answer back and usually with a solid argument to back it. The fact that money needs effort and hard work, which parents do the entire day, needs to be understood and acknowledged by her.

I made some mental notes of the points I would put forth for mutual discussion. Also, I thought about ideas for convincing for accepting a minimum increase, if at all in pocket money. When it is about their pocket allowance, kids don't lag in calculations even if weak in mental maths. They can very well calculate their expenses as per the amount decided and put forward their views for more. Say you make a pact for rupees 500 per month; it will not take long for them to make a list of their spending and prove the amount to be atrociously low. I smiled as I recollected the past few such interactions.

I thought of reminding her about all the expenses she does 'not' make, though should come from her pocket money like gifts for her sis and us; she treats her friends that get subsidised by her dad. How not to compete with her friends to throw treats now and then. I planned to offer her multiple times increase in the pocket money if she was willing to spend on everything from it.

There was one thing I thought of insisting on Tiara; it was to maintain a written account of all the money received and spent. I hope this idea will help her use her money judiciously. She should have a hang of the amount she has in hand and plan her expenses accordingly. She would learn her lesson well without any bitter feelings for her parents. She needs to understand that her parents aren't miser; they want her to be frugal. She must not be a spendthrift but appreciate the value of money.

She needs to understand that gradually kids must inculcate the thought to earn money and be self-dependent. It will help them build the idea of putting in hard work and make a bright future! I keep reminding my kids that they need to work hard to have a luxurious life. Once they know that it takes dedication, sweat, and work to make money, and the reason why we call it 'hard earned', they will value it for sure. I was all set to face Tiara when she returned from school with my brilliant plan in place. But what happened was beyond my imagination, and Tiara delivered a googly which had me clean bowled!

Value for money by Teens

I was all set to leave for school. I was so excited as it was just ten days to go for my birthday. Also, I was supposed to get my increased pocket money as promised the previous year and my b'day allowance today evening. I thought of better reminding mom before leaving so that she does forget to withdraw cash. As I reminded her, pat came the reply, "We will discuss it!" The smile faded from my face. Oh my, so will it be another year without an increase. And then I thought of the plan I already had in place. Mom would be in for a shocker when I returned, I thought with a twisted smile. I was now even more determined to achieve an increase in my pocket allowance, come what may!

My day went well so did my class test. I was looking forward to meeting Mom and just hoped that Dad too gets delayed for his lunch and is there to listen to my plea when I make my case for an increase in my pocket money.

My prayer seemed almost answered as I found Dad too when I entered home. Mom greeted me with a bit extra enthu than usual. I asked dad to wait since I had something important to discuss. He responded that he had a talk with mom and was looking forward to discussing my pocket money.

We sat down after I had my lunch. Dad and Mom both started by telling me about our previous year's lengthy talk on the value of money. They reminded me how I had readily agreed to pay heed to that discussion. I politely interrupted them and requested them to hear me out before going any further. And here is how I clean bowled my parents, I said:

Do you people realise in the past one year I have become very prudent in my shopping? Unlike my so many friends, I have stopped asking for products from my favourite brands. Whether it is about the nail polishes at Accessorize, junk jewellery at Clair's, pencil case at 'Smiggle', or the sports shoes at Nike, I do not ask for them anymore. Be it anything, small or big, I look for a quality product and not necessarily for the brand. I also accept that mom never hinders me when once in a while, I opt for them. She never imposes her choice on me too.

I shared with them my moulded thought process while shopping:

1. Why buy this when I have a similar one.

2. It is no longer embarrassing if I walk out of the store after glancing at everything and not buying anything. It is a different me altogether.

3. I do not buy another pair of denim for its new shade of blue, etc., only because they are a year old.

4. I look for reasonably priced brands to buy. I have started to understand money does not grow on trees.

5. I do not buy books if I can find them on my Kindle.

6. Last but not least I have started enjoying window shopping too.

Both my parents were looking at me with confusion reigning on their faces. Dad asked me what was I getting at? They were happy to note these changes in me but could not link this with the increase in my allowance! I replied, "You people had promised last year that if I begin to understand the value of money, my monthly allowance shall go up." I urged them to consider the changes in me I listed out and appraise whether or not I now know the worth of money.

I further told them what I have secretly been doing for the past year:

1. I have stopped giving a treat to friends on a whim,

2. I ceased to buy a new dress just because my BFF bought it

3. I stopped frequent demands for new phone handset

4. I stopped surfing Amazon and other online shopping sites. I do not get lured into buying unnecessary things.

5. I stopped get carried away for excess shopping only because something is in trend,

and then I dropped the bombshell:

I am saving money, and I have put aside INR X in the last 12 months.

Wow! Never saw such a look on my parents, totally zapped, happy, bewildered. They both got up in surprise and hugged me. There is more to come. "Mom, Dad, now that I have proved to you people that I have fully understood the value of money, I trust you shall have no hesitation in doubling it this year."

I also told them about my plans of building my own small business, which would help me earn some money. I will discuss its elaborate plan with mom.

Guys, I am happy that I understood the value of money in time, maybe just a wee bit late, but better late than never. Mom never says 'No' for spending, just emphasises on saving too. Now I have understood that the best and safe way of doubling your money is to fold it over once and put it in your pocket, in short, make savings (Rather than spending it unnecessarily) And on a parting note would like to quote Oscar Wilde on money: "When I was young, I thought that money was an important thing in life; now that I am old, I know that it really is. -Oscar Wilde."

CHAPTER -15

ACADEMICS

The most crucial part of a student's life

When I started writing this chapter, I was not very clear about its content. I feel all the topics I have touched on in various chapters have a crucial impact on a teen's academic performance. Be it discipline, time management, nutrition, habits even bullying. So, I thought of writing something that directly impacts their learning and is so close to home: We parents!

Before I narrate a specific incident, let me share my take on teens and today's academics.

If we feel our kids are struggling academically, we try all within our means and beyond to bring them back on track. Ultimately, we resort to begging, nagging, bargaining, and punishment, mostly all of which is often in vain. We need to discern the root cause or causes of their poor performance. Teens face academic challenges for a variety of reasons. The issue may be as simple as vision problems or other external factors like physical ailments, conflict at home, poor diet, insufficient sleep, fight with a friend, a new crush or bullying, or excessive screen time. If your child's time is spread too thin with extracurricular activities and friend commitments, their schoolwork is bound to suffer. At times your child's problems may be internal. Learning disorders, some mild mental illnesses are all common causes for the academic struggles of tweens and teens. Emotional, mental, and similar conditions often go undiagnosed in some adolescents and teens. For many parents, problems in school are the first clue that something may be wrong. Fortunately, these problems are usually easily identifiable and addressed when we understand the underlying cause. I must add that the issues change almost completely near mid-teens, i.e., 16 and above.

A friend suggested sending away teens to a hostel or a residential school who struggle at school. Her logic was that children receive the help they need emotionally and mentally while attending school and enjoying social and recreational opportunities. There shall be an environment where teens feel safe and supported and can focus on academics. Though she was convincing, what kept nagging at me was why not provide the same opportunity to teens at home? Things became clearer; my belief was firm in this regard when this incident happened.

I have been happy-go-lucky in the case of academics of Tiara. She has been an above-average student and has always been doing her things all by herself. I did not have to do much apart from guiding her for a few things until junior school. She was a trouble-free child when it came to studies but had issues in some areas.

As was explained to me by my parents, I hold a different view about education and studies. I was never spoon-fed and was always encouraged to be attentive in class and do the homework myself. Similarly, I advocated for both my kids to finish their homework on their own; they must ask their teacher in school when in confusion. I believe the home task is a way for the teacher to judge a student's level of understanding. It acts as general feedback to the teacher for her teachings in the class. However, my not assisting them in their work was not taken kindly by them. They felt sad, scared, and unhappy about it. Usually, when denied my help, they both would react with welled-up eyes and silence.

One day I saw her on the verge of tears, and her discomfort was obvious. I gently inquired what was bothering her. She just gave me a blank stare and left the room without uttering a word. All I could hear was the banging of her room's door, which she must have slammed. I waited for her inner storm to calm down and went to her room after a while. She had cried, which was evident from wet streaks on her face. Before I could even ask, she said it was difficult to cope with a few subjects. She could not understand them in school and was unable to handle her homework by herself. She feared that her teacher might scold her, and then those particular things could lead to her poor performance. Being a good student, she was even concerned about not winning the excellence card.

It was the first time I found that she had fear for academics and was under peer pressure. She went on speaking of her concerns one by one. I feel it shall be best understood by parents when hearing it directly from her. Honestly, it was an eye-opener for me, so over to Tiara!

Academics @ Teens

Be in any subject the problems are many. I am always stuck while doing Mathematics. "Problems are always problematic, phew!" It was a day before the Maths exam; as usual, I forgot everything that I had practiced for so long. After trying to solve it twice, my mind always says to give up. I always feel that I will not be able to do it anyway. Thus, no point wasting time over it, and I move on to the following sum. But gosh! The next seems the same. The best thing I feel was that I must ask Alexa to solve the sums for me; the questions are from the previous year's test papers of which I do not have the solutions. After hunting on google, a few videos here and there, I managed to solve 75% of the exercise. By the end of the day, I was confident my final score would be around 60-65 %. Anyhow, even after having confidence, a fear cloud hovered in my mind making me nervous enough. My tears stood at the brim, ready to set off in motion. The worst thing that could happen was that my mom was right at the dining table, and she witnessed every move of mine. I was sure her hawk eyes would not miss my welled-up eyes. I did what was easiest and quickest to do to avoid any enquiry from her. I rose up and quietly went inside my room. In a hurry, the door closed a bit loudly. I tried to hold back my tears anyways, they still did not stop, and I had no way to prevent myself from not being fearful. My fearful emotions gave a sudden push, and the dam of my tears broke with all possible sobbing noises. I lost control and failed to stop myself, making it evident for mom to hear me.

Mom entered the room. She had a genuine concern written all over her face. She felt sad for me and assured me that she was there to give ears to my woes. She encouraged me to share all my issues be they big or small. I am so happy that God gave me the courage to speak my mind and share all my problems with Mom, who sat there so lovingly holding my hand. I must say that her physical loving touch was a booster for me to share without fear.

I told her what worried me was my lack of complete preparation leading to poor marks in my exam. My friends would call me a loser for not getting excellent marks which I mostly do. I also might lose my other topper friends as they might look down upon me. My biggest fear was no longer remaining the teachers' pet. Mom was all ears, listening very attentively. I then blurted out something that had been going on in my mind for a long. I said, "You and Dad never have time for me. Whenever I ask for help, you shoo me away". I was startled at my own words, and so was mom. Her bewilderment was glaringly visible on her face. I wondered whether my momentary emotional outburst was wrong!? I waited with bated breath for her outburst, which never came. She hugged me and murmured, "Baby, I am so sorry, it must have happened unintentionally." She urged me to share more of my concerns and what made me say what I just did. Her 'cool' reaction gave me enough confidence to share with her things that constantly nagged my mind. "You never help me with my homework!" I told her the pressure that I get from both her and dad about my result and that they were more bothered about my friend's marks than me. Also, they ask me about the class performance and compare my marks with the highest scorer. I felt as if they were more interested in knowing about the class (especially my close-knit friend group) and discussing their progress rather than mine. I confessed that at times when I felt embarrassed about not scoring marks at par with her friends.

Mom was equally forthcoming too. She candidly accepted that she needed to introspect, and maybe they had probably not given me enough quality time. She almost apologised and at the same time assured me that they do care for me and I could completely bank on them.

I smiled and said that I was happy she heard me out with love and patience, even for understanding my issues. I tried to take advantage of the moment and said, "Mom, I'm sure you will consider helping me with my home task now!" I thought I had her pinned, but she is Mom after all. She added with full enthusiasm, "Sure, dear! While we are at it, how about discussing the other things that hinder your academics. Let us list them out too!" So, the ball was back in my court. We talked at length, and the outcome was this list:

- Lack of discipline

- Laziness

- Procrastination

- Low confidence

- No practice

- Zero concentration

- Screen time etc.

She reminded me of the fights with friends that take a lot of my time, energy and it spoils my mood too. Tiffs will take place, but I needed to keep them away from intruding into my academics.

We continued to chat for some more time, and she confided how she felt about my performance and that I was way better in many other aspects than the kids of my age.

She confessed that grades were crucial for parents, but she also added that they aren't the only essential lessons to be learned. The school performance alone cannot be a measure of their success. She said this pressure of academics is a normal one and can be a temporary setback for many. In conclusion, while caressing my cheek, she said, "..and her daughter was no exception". It brought a broad smile to my face.

Her words delighted me. She assured me a new leaf would turn soon, not only in my studies but also in my relationship with my parents. I had the assurance that my parents were with me and all I had to do is perform for myself. I did not have to compete with others anymore. I needed to compete with 'self' and be just a wee bit better than yesterday! I felt relieved and was sure to have a good night's sleep. The pessimism in me found a way out of me. I definitely have academic pressures, but now I shall happily walk on my path with my parents!

CHAPTER-16

PROCRASTINATION

It's Sunday late evening, and the clock was ticking. Tiara was writing frantically, doing a task to be submitted in school the next day. She was trying to complete it before bedtime while muttering to herself for not starting it sooner. "Why did this happen again?" "Where I went wrong?" "Why do I lose my focus repeatedly?"

It looked like a familiar sight! Well, you're not alone. Most parents of teens or nearby age have to view this 'often repeated' distressing sight helplessly. The answer to the many questions that cropped up in Tiara's mind is one: She is in the habit of procrastination, just like so many more in her age group.

Before we move further, let us understand what procrastination is?

Procrastination is the habit of delaying a task, usually an important one while focusing on less urgent, more enjoyable, and simple activities instead. It is important to note that it is very different from laziness, which is more about being lethargic or unwilling to act.

As a mother of a tween and a teen, I will tell you that procrastination is a word that carries with it a lot more than its dictionary meaning. It brings some dangerous elements such as stress and anxiety, leading to anger.

This attitude of delaying things that the teens develop is worrisome. This habit can prove to be a hindrance in the long run; and can be, if not irreversible, a tough one to overcome. I must also add that procrastination blows the routine and time-management to bits.

I'm sure my detailed view on procrastination is not needed for you to get an idea of what I must be going through with my kids, as most of us are in the same boat. Every time a work is assigned, they mostly agree to do it but say:

"Yes, mum, give me a while, and I shall do it."

"I'll do that after finishing my serial."

"Okay, I shall finish one round of my game and then do it."

"Mom, I shall do it after a nap of 10 minutes" (Naps are not generally short & 'snooze' time is a different story altogether)

Always having this 'I will do it later' attitude causes irritations. This syndrome is growing among the kids of today and is a known cause for worry.

Procrastination is unhealthy at any time but pinches more severely when its cumulative effect of the entire week falls on a weekend. Sunday is a fun day and relaxing day for everyone, including us mothers. With no worries for school uniform, tiffin, or early breakfast, it is a morning to chill and allows late wake up. Though morning is lazy and relaxing, the rest of the day is more than usual work, as husband and kids are all at home. I find less time for myself which I otherwise give to my writing and other stuff. I am sure it happens with most of the homemakers like me, especially on a Sunday. Thus, whether it is a weekday or a weekend, nothing works without time management. However, to deal with the weeklong mess made out of books, board games, dressing knick-knacks, socks, sports shoes, and so many things that need to be kept back in their assigned places, throw a spanner in the works. These things may seem trivial but needs lots of time. A little help from their side, doing these small chores without procrastination, can save the house from chaos and stupid debates. A common proverb: 'Prevention is better than cure' is so meaningful indeed. Read on to get a better picture of what I want to express.

Not all Sundays are just the same. This Sunday, the 'spanner' was a bigger one! Tiara suddenly remembered she had her grades of two subjects the next day and had not studied the entire week. It was not a surprise test. She knew about it well in advance. Gosh! It meant a complete working Sunday for me too. Maybe the entire week, she got no time due to homework though that too is not true. She could easily schedule the revision for Friday evening or the next day but wasted Saturday and the night before. She watched DIY videos and finished all episodes of her favourite serial, not to mention texting and selfies. Needed stuff was untraceable, so then followed the hunt of the misplaced books and stationery items that messed up the entire study room. To rub salt on the wound, she received a reminder to join a Zoom meeting of friends in an hour. "Mom! I will revise later!" She urged and assured me she would manage. Can you beat that? She even refused to study for the hour which was spare between then and the meet. It was not the kind of Sunday I was looking ahead. But I had no option but to give her my time.

I ask her to keep learning her lessons and do revisions in advance; so that she can remain calm (me too) and spend time normally, even during her exam days. I have always tried to explain that finishing her studies in time will give her ample time for simple revision just the night before the exams. But it is a familiar scenario to see her not do the needed tasks beforehand. When things are done timely, they become more fruitful and satisfactory, which she does not realise.

I'm sure that many parents like me will agree that they too have been facing similar problems with their kids often. I fail to understand that when there is homework assigned on a Friday that needs submission by Monday, why is it not taken up before Sunday night? The project work that comes with a deadline is taken up only the evening before the submission day. The panic comes with the things needed for the project work. They go hunting for their materials which are for sure not kept in the places meant to be. Then follows the rush to the stationery store to buy the rest of the items. The printings and photocopy work stand in the queue. There are times when their mind suddenly wakes up to say that they need black track pants for their annual function, which happens to be the next day.

Weekdays are no exception. Procrastination can raise its head anytime. It was a usually hectic day, and the couch in the drawing-room did not allow Tiara to leave. That is how I tease her when she sits with laid back attitude in front of the TV - that poor Tiara cannot get up as the Sofa is holding her back. Her ultimate mode of entertainment, which is the ' idiot box ', kept her audio-visual senses glued till it was late evening. She suddenly realised some of her incomplete tasks for the next day and sprang out of the couch. Coming out of the lazy mode with stooping shoulders, she asked me how I managed all the days' works on time. This question coming from her was quite interesting and showed she had some concern for herself. I wanted to help her out as usual hence I showed her my weekly schedule and explained that I make the same a week in advance. I explained to her that finishing the task on the same day, in time, reduces workload as well as last-minute panic. She should also maintain an organiser and fix up her timings for the particular tasks to be done. She did make an organising chart, but that was meant more for decorative purposes only. It got pinned up on the soft board and got lost among other crafts which were on display.

'Time management' is the last thing teens ever comprehend. No matter how many lectures you give them, or calmly explain to them the judicious use of time, they never understand; it all seems to fall on deaf ears! They have mastered the art of time wastage. They do things that should not happen at that particular hour. It gets strenuous to make them do the required activities that are need of the hour. They are pretty irritating to deal with and can test your patience now and then. Hopefully, you are getting it. Phew!

I don't know how much is she going to follow the idea? I was happy that she realised that some action was needed to overcome procrastination and make her life easier. I hope she follows certain principles in her life and uses her time more efficiently without putting the things in the pending folder all the time.

Nevertheless, to drive my point home, I ensured Tiara Googled the word *procrastination* and checked a few definitions and meanings. It seemed to work well.

Please Chill! Says the teen

Almost at gunpoint, Mom made me check the word Procrastination on Google. Honestly, it was a life-changer. I will come to it later, but here is what I was like before that.

Let me recount a typical weekend of mine. It was Friday evening; I clearly remember I have a quiz on Monday and need to copy a poem and draw some biology diagrams. I calculated that I have almost two and a half days to do them. Chill! I told myself. I continued to watch television the entire weekend. Mom's reminders went in one ear and out the other; the in-between 'portion' was busy watching favourite shows. I listened to music and texted friends till late at night and woke up very late. I started my morning with my headphones on with blasting music. My laptop was my companion that let me play my favourite songs as mom asked me not to play loud music. Then the television attracted me to entertain my audio-visual senses so much that I spent time lying on the couch, which mom calls my enslaver. I love to refer to ' Do It Yourself ' videos on YouTube that update me about the various trending crafts, so I almost binge-watch them. Anyway, weekends are to chill!

I don't know how but just a while back, it was Friday evening, and suddenly, Sunday afternoon was upon me, and I was unaware. While I was lazing on the couch, my classmate called up to ask for some help in bio diagrams. Bio diagrams? What was she talking about? My mind did not immediately register, and with that rang a 'gong' in my mind.

The realisation of several things happened simultaneously, and suddenly that I found myself in panic. I shouted at Anya to hunt for my Bio book. I looked for my Shakespeare book, as there was a class test the next day. Someone was running to fetch me my poem book because I was supposed to copy it in my homework copy. The biology diagrams were incomplete. It was already Sunday afternoon, and I was in a hot soup. In school, my teachers would get fire at me, and I was sure to face harsh consequences. These thoughts made me start doing my pending work frantically while introspecting why I repeated mistakes.

I realised that spending two days doing different non-studies activities and wasting time watching the screen was not worth it. I was punished in the school for incomplete work and also had to face embarrassment. I could have been a little more active and off-screen to finish all my work and present myself with confidence and pride. The laid-back attitude of mine time and again put me in a situation that was indeed shameful. The shame I faced at school was in my mind too, and I realised that I could have made better use of the weekend rather than sticking to the couch for movies and serials. Along with weekend chilling I could have done things that kept me busy and were productive otherwise.

I walked towards mom to ask her something I had never cared to ask before. "How do you manage to do all the work in time?" I asked her. She looked at me, and her radiant smile told me that she was feeling quite happy that I was concerned about myself. She took my hand and made me sit beside her. We talked at length about my habits in general and procrastination in particular. She then shared how she made a list of 'to do things' a week in advance. She showed me her latest list so neatly prepared, and the work completed duly ticked. Excitedly I said, "Mom, both our worries, will be over soon." She further advised, "Just making an organiser will not be enough. You will need to follow it diligently." Then she reminded me of an incident that made me blush and lower my head. She said, "Remember when you had grades in 2 subjects the next day, and you forgot. You were about to sit for the revision when your friend's reminder came for a Zoom meeting starting in an hour. You pleaded before me to commence the studies after the meet. The reminder to you that you still have an hour to study did not find favour with you. So, you see, I acted as your 'organiser', reminded you, even coaxed you, but it did not work. Do you think an inanimate object like an Organiser alone shall be of any help!!?? More than the Organiser, it is 'you' who matter! You have to work proactively and with rock-solid discipline."

She insisted that before starting on the organiser thing, I must Google the word procrastination, read its meaning and definition and try relating to them. She insisted that I spend a minimum of 30 minutes on it. She demanded that I give her feedback at the earliest.

It changed everything. I exceeded the mandated 30 minutes and continued much longer. At so many places, I almost felt as if this word was coined for me. Guys, I suggest that each one of you must do this 'exercise', and spend some time with the word - Procrastination. I made some bullet points that I share below. You can make your list.

01. Recognise that you are procrastinating.

02. Make efforts to understand the 'why' of this habit of yours.

03. Don't beat yourself for this bad habit; forgive yourself.

04. Always keep a 'to do list' handy

05. Ask Mom up front to keep a check on you. You can share your schedule with her. I suggest a few of your close friends can have a 'similar' routine and you can check on each other. It will also mean having free time at the same hour so you can text or chat without remorse.

06. Rewiring your internal dialogue helps too. We mostly tell ourselves, "I need to or have to do this task!" It implies a sort of pressure. Start telling yourself: I choose to do my bio drawings NOW! Well, now it is your choice.

07. Sharing a phrase that I came across, I loved it: "Eat an elephant beetle" first thing in the morning. Don't do it literally- yuck! Lolz! It means to do the strenuous tasks at the earliest as these are the ones that we defer and fall into the pit of postponing things.

I got the idea about creating an organiser from Mom, and I tried to work on it with a twist. I decided to look for an app that could make my work simpler by giving me reminders. I even weighed the consequences. I contemplated if it was a bad idea because the reminder would make me look into the screen now and then. Would it lure me to using the phone for other purposes? I repeated mom's words aloud, "It is you who matter!" I promised myself to be disciplined and went ahead and created my first weekly schedule on the organiser diary. I shared it with mom. I would add to the idea by segregating the most important one and putting up a paper on the pinboard listing them in bold so that the same is in my eyes regularly.

Okay, I got this right, and here is what I finally decided

1. List – Make a list of things to do for the entire week. A set reminder not more than thrice in a day.   Be willing and finish off the work as required and enjoy life.

2. Schedule – A timetable schedule for the daily tuitions and classes is a good idea. Make a routine with days and time along with the name of the activity and refer to it daily. Along with it, you can divide your time for studies, play, screen, and craft. You will find that you have much more time in hand to do more of what you want to do. Most importantly, it will help bring down your unlimited screen time to maybe an hour every day. But yes, you need to check your schedule when reminded and don't just snooze; follow it religiously.

3. Be attentive, be active –Keep your ears open while watching TV so that you can hear your mom call out to you when it is time to switch it off. You will not be able to move your butt out of the couch initially unless reminded by her.

4. Indulge in something productive and feel good about it.

5. My grandpa (Nanu) suggested me this, and I found it super helpful.: At the end of the day, while reviewing what you accomplished, do also make a small note of the accumulated time you actually spent on things such as TV, Texting, Music, lazing during the day, and review it weekly to realise whether you are well within your set limit or any tweaking in it is needed.

So, I am on my way to get rid of procrastination. Do you also wish to? If yes, do it now! Drop the book, pick up your phone (don't text me!), and create your work schedule NOW!

CHAPTER – 17

COMMUNICATION GAP

I skipped writing an incident in this chapter related to its heading 'Communication-Gap' as I found there are numerous trivial ones. Over a period, these petty ones start a crack which widens to a gap.

My parents and I had a generation gap but never a communication gap. Yes, we had different perspectives for so many things and differed on many. But most of the time, we found a middle path sheer through communication. I started off well with my kids; they were a chatty lot. After the school got over, both of my girls would call me up from the car itself. Unable to even wait to reach back home, they used the chauffeur's phone to narrate to me how good or bad the day happened to be, and it would continue as they entered home. In my time, I would also start talking while opening my shoes as I entered home. My mom had to quieten me as she served me lunch. Their stories and my stories were so similar. Beginning from what good or bad the teacher did,

fight with a friend;

what friends brought in the lunch box that they loved to eat;

their marks if any;

experience at the school lab;

something that happened outside the school while waiting for the car, and so much more. This similarity, I found in their school stories with mine, at times made me wonder blissfully, "Seems we don't have a generation gap." They would happily answer my queries and fill in the gaps in their narration when asked for. We seemed to be flawlessly communicating.

The euphoria did not last long. Now, when one is a teen and the other a tween, they hardly volunteer to talk about their day. Even on asking about their day spent, they get irritated and very casually reply, "Ok" or "Like any other day", "A normal day, mom." Their gestures and replies so candidly convey why do I bother to enquire about anything at all?

One afternoon I overheard a conversation; if only we can call it one, there were hardly any words to express meanings or feelings. That conversation was something like Ok... Hmm... I see... Alright... Umm... Omg... yes... cool... Aww... Haha... Pich(sound). It was Tiara's side of the chat.

What kind of a silent talk was this in which only the other person spoke!? This was a general conversation happening between none other than she and her close friend. Do not assume they have such telepathy that not many words were needed to express what they wanted to say. I noticed that this monosyllabic, crisp talk with more sounds than words happened when I come within a hearing distance... lol

The use of short and abrupt words has taken over her long and ongoing conversations. At times, I wanted to plug my ears to it, and how much the silence pinches me today is unexplainable. I wonder where that communication got lost? Why is there nothing to talk to parents about when they got back from school, while there is so much still to share with the friends; with whom they had spent time their entire day? The free evenings before and after homework are also for their friends, so when is the time for us? "Has the generation gap commenced?" I wondered.

I also realise that the only long conversations we have these days are of arguments and silly debates. Any words from me that do not match their frequency becomes a problem. Life is more about confrontations for every single bit of instruction. She justifies everything as she thinks she is never wrong. A counterargument is always ready, be it about a messy room or unfinished meal. She says she is grown up, that's alright, but then I expect some maturity, right? "No!! Wrong.", says my subconscious. I need to fathom where am I erring?

Why does every word I utter to explain actually turn into a fight? Every second sentence falls into a heated debate. Where have the long chatty conversations gone? I doubt if she now remembers what discussions mean. Why she hardly wants to hear anything that does not suit her temperament. Deaf is not the word, but she practices selective hearing and seems to go out of the conversation the moment she wants to. Why?! Is my knowledge about child psychology outdated? Seems their minds have changed like the upgrading technology.

Everything that I ask or tell her has a short reply, an excuse, few rude words, or nothing at all. Excuses are the only explanations I get from her. The girl who used to fill up the room with smiles and laughter has nothing to speak about now. All her stories and fun talks were quite entertaining. I need them all back, and I need a way to bring them back again. I want her ' old self ' back. Is it what I see a '6' where I stand is actually a '9' from her angle? So, what is the solution? How do I reduce the widening 'generation gap'? We need to understand each other's perspectives, and as a parent, I must take the initiative. I so clearly understood but somehow seemed to have forgotten that the 'generation gap' is nothing but a 'communication gap' between people of different generations. It was evident that this communication gap between kids and us happened because we took things for granted. Our failure to convey properly; or understand the information, intent, meaning of what was said by the kids or vice versa had led to this gap. An easy way to remember how to avoid this is to keep in mind the 5T's: Time, Talk, Tenderness, Touch, and Trust are the keys to both the heart and mind of kids helping bridge gaps between them and parents.

Here are a few (there are sure to be many others) causes of the generation gap between parents and child for which we need to apply some remedy at the earliest:

1. Paucity of Understanding

The reason is not far to find. No two generations speak the same language. Compared to the days when parents were growing up to what it is now, their way of thinking and what one deems simple is weird for the other.

2. Mistakes-Intolerance

Many parents do not disregard or tolerate mistakes. They rebuke and berate their kids out of proportion. We all know that kids need to make mistakes and learn from them as they grow in life. However, if they get reprimanded, it will widen the distance and create a situation where there is no communication for 'monosyllables".

3. Similarities

Many parents expect their offspring to be their replicas. Some parents even dream on behalf of their kids. They compel kids towards their choice of direction, having minimal concern for kids' desires.

4. Comparisons

Comparing siblings to each other or even with their friends or own friend's or neighbour's kids is a vital cause for the gap growing wider. This makes them lose self-confidence and can shatter any enthusiasm they had.

5. Absence of Interaction

With the stress that comes from work, homemaking, and the responsibilities of the adults, parents often find themselves too weary spending time with their kids every day. And the time they try to squeeze out lacks quality and seems more like a compulsion. This leads to a lack of communication and interaction that widens the generation gap.

Communication is a crucial aspect of character building, sharing a healthy relationship, harmony in the family, and so much more. There are many ways in which communication can be improved. The counsellors guide through relationship issues, profile building, and even deal with career confusion. Writing a diary can play a prime role in building up communication among parents and children. As said earlier - Timely and proper communication between the two can resolve most issues before they turn into trouble for both! It has to come from both sides; one-sided conversation is no communication. Do refer to the last paragraph of Chapter 2 (Sea-saw of trouble-hood)

When I asked Tiara for her ideas and views about the communication gap, she used an interesting analogy in her reply. She equated parents with the pre windows antiquated computer operating system DOS and projected the teens as Windows 10. Read on. You will love her comparisons and also her suggestions.

While leaving these emotions here, let us hear what Tiara has to say for the same. We might find some solution to better communication or maybe realise where we are going wrong.

Communication-Gap

(Disclaimer: My version is either boring or informative for anyone who is not computer friendly. I insist please read the listed view of what kids desire from parents)

Surprise, surprise, Mom asked for my opinion, my views for something. Wow! It seems I am getting smart. Or is it mummy's some ploy to snare us into doing something which we do not usually readily agree to!!? Anyways, she asked me what my idea was about 'communication-gap, and how to overcome the same? Well, there is no communication gap; it is a generation gap only.

Do you think a DOS-based OS (parents) can handle Windows-based software (teens)? If their 1GB RAM tries to handle 32 GB data, imagine the outcome. The system is sure to crash. So, the option is to reboot...but how many times can you do it...so what is a solution. If they need to read the files created on windows, DOS needs to upgrade to Windows! It is as simple as that. So, I have answered the first part.

Now the second part, how to overcome the same? Well, I said: Upgrade to Windows, but we know that does not happen. What do we do? We need to find a way so that Windows can communicate to DOS and the reverse too. Hmmm... seems as if Mom was correct; it is indeed a communication gap! Trust my analogy must have travelled to the Hard Disk of DOS and understood what I wish to say.

I do not wish to cite examples of disk crashes; there are many blue screens; let me focus on some remedies! All I have listed are from my point of view what we desire from parents.

1. Keep an Open Mind

Windows may be open or be shut; DOS must remain open all the time to read data once a bridge of communication is established between the two. Our way of thinking is very different, may I call it entirely different, from our parents. Parents assume they understand how their child thinks as once upon a time they too were of our age. However, the truth is, parents & teens (DOS and Windows) have no similarity. Their universe and life-style were different than today. Their perspective will be very different, and the contrast can also be appalling for some parents. Somethings that prevail in society now, maybe as trends are easily acceptable to teens, but the same may not have been digestible to parents when they were teens. So keep an openness and not assume that teens *(Windows)* must be just like parents *(DOS)* as outwardly seem identical.

2. Interact

Do not remain static, be proactive. *DOS could do one task at a time, unlike Widows that can multitask.* Parents need to regularly interact with kids and no multitasking while doing it. A simple talk about how their day had gone can be helpful, and you get to know each other. It also gradually makes it easier for both to speak freely too. *Windows need to know they can try to connect with DOS without fear of a Blue Screen.* We kids need to know we can approach our parents with anything and everything. This can ultimately give parents peace of mind since they do not need to worry about their children hiding necessary things. *BTW the DOS is permitted to peek inside Windows.*

3. Listen

When Windows is sending signals DOS must focus on receiving and not attempt to send signals back. Parents must allow their kids time to talk without interruption and listen to what they have to say. Knowing the opinion of teens makes them feel that their desire is also of much importance to Parents. This will also make kids feel much closer to their parents than before. A parent who not only hears but also listens will give kids more encouragement to listen to them.

4. Understand

DOS must at times connect to the same 'port' where Windows connect. Parents must put themselves in their kid's shoes. Add to this attentive listening, and with this connect shall come true-understanding about how kids feel and what they want. If you understand where your child is coming from, you will help you close that generation gap to a large extent.

5. Unconditional Love

DOS should not reject the data just because it is not coming from the same source; they must love it. Love has a way of crossing boundaries and bringing people together, especially parents and kids. Show us how much you love us. The unconditional love and support kids get from parents are very encouraging that they are more inclined to reciprocate. It triggers a 'strong Fevicol bond'!

6. Compromise

DOS may not be able to accept Windows 10 data. The best way is that Windows 10 mellows down to Windows98 and DOS instead of outright rejecting Windows data and agree to accept the watered-down version. People can disagree on things, no matter how close to each other they are. Parents and children are no different. They should not impose their way of thinking on each other; instead, learn to compromise and find a middle path. There are times when parents need to put their foot down with kids, but don't let that foot be unmoving, uncompromising. When parents are a bit flexible instead of dictating every move, kids will get closer to them. This will make the communication gap (which leads to the generation gap) a little smaller.

All said and done, this quote sums it all up about 'gaps': "Each generation imagines itself to be more intelligent than the one that came before it and wiser than the one that comes after it"- George Orwell

CHAPTER - 18

SCREEN SYNDROME

Have you ever heard of Screen Syndrome? No? I'll tell you about it because I probably coined it ☺. I found out that it is not any disorder by birth but acquired later :D People of all ages are susceptible to it, but tweens and teens are more prone to be readily afflicted.

Screen Syndrome happens when different parts of the human body get stimulated only to respond to Screens on Digital gadgets.

The mind uses stimuli of Digital broadcast on TV to focus most;

Palms hold only gadgets be it the palmtop, mobile phone, or the remote control of the TV;

Ears respond only to the digital sound coming from the music box, and eyes stay glued to one screen or the other.

More than these, there are a few other side effects like avoiding serious work, laziness, inattentiveness, boredom, daydreaming, low patience level, and more. Trust you relate to many of these symptoms in your kid.

Multitasking is a revered word in the Corporate-world, but the teens can beat them hands down. Who can watch TV, eat lunch, intermittently scroll while texting and talking with friends as some lovely music is playing!?

The infinite number of hours they can watch the Big-screen and handheld 'small screen' really perplexes me and takes my patience away. It can undoubtedly stop their mind from working, avoiding other important and serious things. Uncontrolled, it can simply ruin their future by making them 'dumb' kids; no wonder TV is called an 'idiot box. The sooner they realise it, the better it would be. Smart Phones are no better, making these kids 'stupid'. The most alarming thing I recently read was that phone addiction might act like a 'gateway drug'!

Soon after their return from school and after lunch would be their TV time. I reluctantly agreed to it because telling them every day to stay away from the TV while having food was not working. To curtail their TV time, I allowed them to watch, only till they finish their lunch. To which I noticed that their appetite grew a bit while their speed reduced. Thus, the screen time extended by an hour or so. Later in the evening, they sit to study if there was homework. To hear songs while texting was necessary to get over the lazy feeling after their occasional nap. Soon the intercom of the house began to ring. It was time to meet her friends, who were waiting at the apartment park. On returning from the playground, their favourite TV show was to begin. Pleading and bargaining ensued for more screen time. With this came promises to make up for the things not done yet; clearing the messy room and study tables, not watching TV the next day, or maybe no TV at dinner time or something else on some other days.

One fine evening which was no different than the usual ones, I decided to be firm and put my foot down at 'NO TV' because it was getting on my nerves. They stay ready to watch their episode with the remote control in hand, cushions tucked in, and eyes glued to the screen. They looked like an actual description of what we call a couch potato; I had two of them with a shade of grumpy faces. I snatched the remote and switched it off without even giving a warning. We had a heated argument. It ended in me losing my cool while they marched off to their study room in a huff. I need not mention it in detail as it is more or less similar in all households with same age group kids.

I knew this was not a remedy, then what was? I tried to note down some pointers and sharing the same.

01. Have patience; it will happen: Try to think of it like toilet training when they were babies – it takes time, ups and downs, teamwork, a sense of humour, and lots of encouragement. I know easier said

than done. Then the 'subject' was not so resisting as they will be now. That's where patience, lots of it, is needed.

02. Alternate activity: Imagine you left a meeting, and in the car, you suddenly find your phone missing! How anxious and strange it feels. Kids would have a similar feeling, probably N number of times stronger when suggested to go 'off screens.' The key is to propose an equally absorbing or even more gripping activity to wean them away. It is still more of a help if you ask them to make their list of 'screen free' activities. It may be easier with tweens but difficult for teens. One thing I am pretty sure about is: they all love spending quality time with their parents. Some researchers have also suggested doing some 'screen' activity together, like playing some multi-player educative or fun games online like Scrabble, Monopoly, Ludo. The rider is, all family members must sit in the same room.

03. Lead by example: Not sure that this works much with tweens and teens as it would with younger ones, but it still helps if you lead by example. When with your children put away your phone as much as possible and reduce your TV time.

04. Tech-Free Time: Having a 'Tech free' mandatory time at a given hour every day for all members and having some gainful or fun activity shall be immensely helpful. Music may be allowed but not earphones, more so at bedtime. Motivate them to read books before sleeping.

05. Family Time: Have some real fun time together. Research, innovate, create activities that can hold all of you for some time. Playing card games find the most favour with kids.

06. Discipline: You need to be firm with routine and not give in to their pleadings. Well, if you remain rigid, the kids will be aware that you will not budge and future fuss reduces or ends.

07. Keep your cool and Communicate: A big task but still do it. At times it pays to take a big breath before doing anything. If nothing else, it shall remove that 'edge' from your voice that 'cuts' them. It helps to be in their shoes momentarily. Before you react, or even respond to their overtime for screens, give yourself 5 minutes to cool down a notch. You may get back to it when you feel more likely to deal with the situation calmly. At the very onset, acknowledge their feeling

of being upset. Do it with a hug before choosing the right words to reprimand. Science tells us that loving touch increases the release of oxytocin, also called the 'cuddle hormone! The words that you utter in this manner would be the most effective communication.

While thinking about a remedy, I realised that I did not follow my recommendations. In the heat of the moment, I lost patience. I did not keep my cool. I was often prone to give in to their bargaining for more screen time, never suggested an alternate activity, etc.

I thought of implementing what I wrote and entered their room with a big smile. Tiara was sitting, seemed to stare into a chasm with a blank face devoid of any expression. I greeted her with a happy face and embraced her lovingly while she was still sitting. Some colour returned to her face and had she smiled back at me. I asserted I should not have been so abrupt and that I am sorry. She looked up at me and conceded that she was rude too and was regretting it. I then asked her to help me help her reduce her screen time as it was getting overwhelming. I sought suggestions from her and assured her that both of us would find a solution. I added that she should proactively consider things from a parent's perspective too. I encouraged her by saying that she was now ~14 and was smart enough to offer solutions.

She did do a grand job. Read on...!

Gadgets – indispensable part of our life!

I am on the edge of the couch, eyes glued to the TV, watching the climax scene of "The London Has Fallen", US president was captivated, and someone held a cutglass against his throat. I seemed to be holding my breath as he gets threatened to be decapitated. The screen goes blank, and then I shout, "Mom!!!!!!" She had snatched the TV remote from my hand and had switched it off. A 'lava' hot argument ensued, and ultimately, I marched out to my study room.

I sat there on my chair with thousands of thoughts running about parents, their aversion for TV and Mobile. I was angry with mommy. I could not overcome a weak voice repeatedly telling me, "Mom requested you to leave the TV and do homework. She is justified in what she did. Maybe you need to apologise!"

Ironically, Mom beat me to it. Not much later, she entered and greeted me with a big smile and held me so lovingly close to her, looked directly into my eyes, and said, "Sorry!" I almost melted in her arms. It took me some effort to hold back my tears. I apologised too and accepted my bad behaviour. We had a heart-to-heart talk at length when mom shared her views about the ongoing issue of Screen abuse. Mom then asked me to share my candid thoughts about my screen time with any gadgets other than ones for educational use. She even asked me to offer my solutions as a teen, keeping parent's point of view in perspective also in this regard.

About today's incident

My first thought: Parents must understand the kids' needs. It is my notion that television is something that helps you unwind yourself. It makes you forget the mishaps of the day. It is relaxing and rejuvenating. It feels like a good day despite having a bad one at school. It may bring back the missing smile due to a bad exam. It may pep up the up environment.

So, is it not crucial to watch TV after school? Don't we have a right to unwind after a hectic day? Can anyone tell the harm in playing on my iPhone? And if there is, then why did they buy me one? My mom is always against TV, she has no interest in TV herself and so finds it a life spoiler, and that is not all; she calls it an idiot Box, and to Sis' a couch potato!

My honest opinion: TV being crucial or helpful in unwinding is just for parents' consumption. Unwinding? We don't get taut when with friends unless there is a tiff; that too is just a ploy to watch TV. TV is at best a distraction. The antics of any comedian are temporary amnesia for the bad events of the day. The moment TV is off, all remain very much there in our minds. We need not forget that whatever little the TV does in eliminating from our mind includes our school lessons of the day.

It is ingrained in my brain that excess of anything is bad, though I mostly ignore the call of my subconscious mind. Mom has minimal interest in Soaps or Sitcoms telecast on TV or YouTube, so she seems to be against TV. I am not. I am all for watching TV but with discipline and time-bound. To my fellow teens, I would strongly suggest keeping a diary of their 'screen time'; simply log in the time we spend before screens other than for studies. If we can do it honestly for just a month, the figures shall astound us and make us rethink deeply, and most of us will end up curtailing it big time.

I wish to share something that might astonish you. It was explained to me by my grandpa nanu. We have 200 days of school every year on average. Study time is ~4 hours per day, and we use around 2 hours studying at home for homework and revision. So in 365 days, we use 200X6=1200 hours gainfully, which is 3.28 hours per day when calculated for a year. Now comes the gripping part. When we reduce just an hour per day of screen time and use it beneficially, that will amount to 'creating' 365 hours from nothing. That is worth 111 days, almost over 3.5 months of valuable work. Imagine living three extra months every year for every 1 hour of reduced screen time. It's an open offer valid for entire school life: 3 months free with 12 months study, no tuition-free applicable. If we get it into our lifestyle can work wonders for life.

Parents having patience is of utmost importance, and I know we test it to the hilt and beyond. I feel when they reach the edge, that's when just a wee bit more of it is required before we succumb to their love and affection.

As suggested by Mom, indulging in screen-free activities that we kids enjoy and with the active participation of parents can be a game-changer.

Identifying our interests or hobbies and pursuing them can act as a reduction in our screen-time. It can also stimulate creative cells in our brain.

It is not for me to say, but parents regularly binge-watch TV or play marathons on gadgets. They give a negative impetus to whatever little resolve we try to garner in curtailing our screen time.

I must confess most of us very fast understand the level of cajoling needed for our parents to give in to our pleadings. It is up to them to remain firm. We would stop whimpering once we understand that you would stand your ground come what may!

Weekly Tech-Free Family Time, be it board or card games, an outing without phones (only emergency calls allowed) can bring radical changes over time.

Last but not least, parent's touch is bliss, more so when we are angry. Add communication with it, which is the mainstay of any relationship, and we are now ready to achieve anything. Communication by parents is vital for us teens to open up and garner the confidence to share things that otherwise accumulate and create stress. Talking things over with an attentive guardian is so calming.

So guys, reduce screen time, live more! Here is a quote I love:

"Time is free, but it's priceless

You can't own it, but you can use it

You can't keep it, but you can spend it

Once you've lost it, you can never get it back."

— Harvey MacKay

CHAPTER – 19

SOCIAL MEDIA

Parents food guide

Food for thought

Not a single article, blog, or book on Teens can be complete without talking about social media at some length.

What we talked about in Chapter no.18, 'Screen Syndrome' was majorly about "Screens" and not social media. One can argue that social media is all about Screen-agreed! But I would rather say that social media is where that screen time leads to via smartphones; now, Smart TVs too (Firestick) are entry gates. If TV and Phones were tobacco, and alcohol- an obsession, then social media is a pure uncut hard drug- an addiction.

The fact is that social media has entered every nook and corner of the Earth. I would rather say social media has its world, the Cyber World where it enslaves its 'netizens.'

Children, tweens, and teens of today strongly connect to social media. They have been growing up in a world so different from the one in which we grew up. We proudly say we did not grow up addicted to playing games on mobile phones or tabs, Facebook or Instagram likes, or followers on YouTube. We need to take this with a pinch of salt, or maybe a handful, because we did not have Facebook or YouTube till 2006 and Insta till 2010. And by then, most of us were already changing the nappies of our kids. In fact, there were no mobile phones in use till I was in standard X. Social media is a new phenomenon, and today's parents do not know how to tackle this newfound 'enslaver' of their kids.

We see our children getting devoured by their addiction to social media. We already talked about some ways to handle their involvement in screens. Rather than asking them to give it up for good, efforts should be of bringing it down to an acceptable level. Stress was also on the need to negotiate, in a way, that it does not become friction between them and us. Handle with love and understanding such that it does not cause unstable relationships or daily conflict. The same is true for social media. Deal it in a way that it becomes a connecting platform. You can make it your tool for a deeper connection with your young ones.

The first step is your acceptance of their relationship with the social media platforms. We parents must understand that our children are growing up in a digital world. Their 'diet' includes social media. With the present pandemic, it has become more of an inextricable part of their lives and ours. It is a fact of life and exists with all of us today; it makes no sense to resist the fact that many parents are addicted to these social platforms.

All the remedies suggested in Chapter 18 for Screens like Alternate activity, Tech-Free Time, Family Time, Discipline, and Communication will also work excellently for social media. Most important shall be 'Walk the talk'!

They must not feel that we are imposing something on them which we do not follow, and actually, it is wrong to do so. We need to be present in the activities of their lives and be with them to replace some part of social media from all our lives. While we are scrolling on Instagram, we say we are working, but while they spend time on their Insta account, we term it a waste of time. Usually, it is not the case with every parent, but things like these are ordinary. Once we learn to spend our time judiciously, it will be easier to teach our kids to do the same. What is unhealthy for them is not healthy for us too. Let us ask ourselves today – how much are we with the kids practically? Are we parents not glued to the screen while having dinner with family, or are we not stuck to our mobiles while traveling in a car, bus, flight or train? If we apply the same analogy here, what Tiara used in Chapter

-18 about time-saving, imagine we shall be living almost 'double lifetime' with our kids!!

Introspect without defending yourself: "How much are we addicted to social media?" Take a moment, sit back and think honestly about your relationship with social media today. The conclusion could be that this habit into our child might have passed on from us! I must hasten to add that there are parents with whom the reverse happened; who were introduced to social media by their kids. Unwittingly, instead of pairing down kids' exposure, they too got captivated by the dreamy world of social media. I advocate all parents of 'ten to teens' must expose themselves to social media without getting hooked on it. It is akin to having an unopened pack of cigarettes and reading the statutory warning about its ill effects. It will give them a clearer idea of the exposure that their kids have. Similar to their kids, a typical thing I found in some parents is the denial factor. They falsely claim, "No way. I am not at all addicted to Social media; I can reduce or stop at will!" It is so similar to many AA participants' claims. They either do not genuinely understand they are addicted or are in self-denial mode. Let me list some tell-tale signs of social media addiction; there may be others:

The first thing you do on waking up after turning off the alarm on mobile is checking social media.

Check N number of times even during the day.

You are irritated when for some reason, you are unable to reach your social media platform.

You are repeatedly checking the 'performance' of your social media post for Likes and Comments.

You start to think more and more about your next post to fetch more Likes & Comments.

You take the ding-dong of your gate as your Message Notification.

You stopped reading books or hearing those Bollywood songs; you prefer social media over your passion for playing chess.

You don't know what that 'green veggi' was on the left side of your plate when asking for a second helping.

So on and so forth...

If any of the above rings a bell, it is time to wake up before it is too late as you need to nudge your kid out of it too, and you cannot do it while asleep.

By the way, this social media is not a threat. We parents must not look at it as a villain only. There are positive aspects too. Both kids and we can learn a thousand things from it, more so after this pandemic. Both my kids easily create some sumptuous dishes by watching them on YouTube without my presence in the kitchen.

Social media is a helpful tool for information, learning, news, and even disaster management as having been proved time and again, more so presently in 2020/21. It is a valuable portal for connection.

Around 1962, almost 60 years back, author McLuhan floated an idea that Mass Communication shall bring the world so close that he coined the term "Global Village." Imagine with the advent of the Internet and Facebook, Twitter, Insta, etc., what do we call a "Global Room"?

Technology in today's world is creating wonders for the human race. It is a vibrant and fertile digital platform for worldly connection bringing people closer.

Let us be street smart in the cyber world. May I say let us be "Social Smart"! Be fully aware of how we can be role models for our children, and mould them to create healthy individuals -physically, mentally, and socially. We must strive to use social media and other trending applications to that effect. "Catch them young" works wonders here. Although it is a tough job and time-taking also; but in the end, children will very well absorb the correct way. They will learn the usage of the media in a positive manner rather than in an addictive way.

It is a love triangle, social media: Kids: Parents! Don't let social media win. Swamp them with your love, quality time, and so much so that they hardly notice their reduced time on social media.

For Teens: Think before you eat.

It's a known metaphor, "You are what you eat." I added a few more words to it to make it more relevant here: "You are what you eat, and so is your brain!"

Teens: Junk Fast Food Menu	
Items	Junk Ingredients
Facebook/Insta depression	Made to feel inferior, Inability to fit in, and unaccepted by friends.
FB/Insta/Youtube/Snapchat anxiety	Getting fewer comments awaiting Likes or for unbroken Snap Streak.
Cyberstalking	Smartphones can give away your actual location.
Cyberbullying/Public Shaming	Post false, embarrassing, or hostile info' about you.
Reduced Sleep	Worry about what friends are posting and sharing. Effort to be first to Like /Comment.
Lower Self-Esteem	Fall into pit comparing peer's posts and reels highlighting best moments, usually false.
Social Isolation	Videos posted of uninvited parties. FOMO. Loss of face.
Fake Friends	With a race to have more friends, you collect many fake, who misuse data/photos.
Unwise/Illogical Expectations	Everyone lies on SM. You build castles in the air looking at unauthentic activities on SM.
Human touch is lost	Busy with Smart Phone when waiting, be it doc's chamber; or a queue or in bus or train and miss a chance to interact with people.

Decreased physical activity	Binge surfing: No time for outdoors
Internet addiction	Physical ailments, neck pain, eye strain, poor grades

Teens Organic (Healthy) Food Menu	
Items	Benefits
Face Time, Zoom: Staying connected with family n friends worldwide: College/Hostel	Bonding strengthens
Google, Explorer, Safari, etc	Easy access to Info and research.
Learning skills: Video Tutorial, DIY videos, Udemy,	Economical, comfortable, and lessons are easily repeatable.
Online School and Tuitions	Saving commuting time
Fundraising, Social awareness	Easier to get involved in Social Work
Outlet of Creativity	Appreciation encourages
Online Guidance	Easy to get mentored
Life-Long staying in touch	Moving from one city to another does not matter
Teaching SM to Parents and Grandparents	Feel empowered spreading knowledge
Learn more about new things, cultures, etc.	Broadens outlook
Expressing your ideas to more people	Boost in self-confidence, Helps introverts too.
Getting latest information	Staying updated
Faster and easy Communication	Have miniaturised the world from Global Village to Cyber Room

Well, guys, it's a love triangle here too, Junk:Teens:Organic! In your language -Flirt with Junk but stay bonded with Organic!

CHAPTER- 20

TASKS FOR TEENS

Journey into your mind

You disagree with your parents in many things; your perception does not match their idea, which is okay. Yet to not let the difference of opinion take the shape of an argument, there needs to be thorough thinking. The next moment when you are peaceful and alone, take a walk into your mind and rediscover yourself.

Imagine yourself on a path where you are going to discover your inner self. Go on this journey to find out more about yourself. Think of your attitude with yourself as well as with others. Write down whatever you feel about yourself, judge yourself, and make confessions too.

Leap from confusion to confidence

Taking the task of self-introspection is a commendable job in itself. Not everyone dares to take up this one. Attitude is all about confidence. It is about charming everyone, not only your best friend but also other friends, your parents, and your teachers. Use your power of communication and good gestures to build strong connections and bonds.

Why not ask yourself a few general questions to get rid of confusion and discover your confidence level?

Q. Do you get embarrassed quickly?

Q. Are you outgoing?

Q. Do you make friends easily?

Q. Do you get nervous while answering or reading in the class?

Q. Are you comfortable dancing at parties?

Q. Is it tough to make new friends?

Q. Do you blush when someone compliments?

Q. Would you cry if you perform poorly in your exam?

Q. Are you too shy to talk to anyone new?

Q. Is it hard to stand up for yourself?

Q. Do you feel embarrassed to hug your parents in front of your friends?

Maybe you need brushing up somewhere for the betterment of the skills you already possess.

To be confident and have a great attitude, you need to know yourself inside out. The facts about you will help you become better. You must also care to know about people close to you to develop a good bond with them.

How about knowing your parents?

How much do you know about your mom? You know her life from after you came into existence. She had a different life before she brought you into this world. Have you ever asked her about the things she has loved to do throughout her teenage? She might surprise you by sharing the most outrageous things she would have done in her youth. Her real-life stories could prove to be the best confidence booster; you never know! Ask her about the restrictions she faced and the most importantly, how did she cope up! Interesting, isn't it?

Dad can prove to be the real hero of your life. But for that, you need to know him inside out. His interest and hobbies might have got buried under a mountain of responsibilities. He might have lost the compassion of playing his favourite sport because of the worries which take a toll on him. Go ahead and help them reach out to their childhood.

Once you have explored their hidden life stories, you can try out ways to make them happy by making them do things they like to. Do you enjoy playing the DARE game? Did I hear a YES? I have an idea! Teach your parents and make them do cool dares (wink).

You can play it with yourself too. Yes, make a list of things to achieve this week and get started. Give yourself simple dares on the first level. It could be anything simple, say trying out a new kind of fruit – Have you heard of an apple, yea? But you have never had it right! Just kidding, of course, try eating an apple religiously despite you disliking it. It's a simple yet great idea to keep yourself healthy and your mum happy.

Do you come out of your shell when among new people? Dare the things you usually do not do and bring yourself out of your comfort zone. Try out a conversation.

Ever given a thought to your unwanted attitude? Re-think how your attitude affects you, your friends, your family, and others. See if you need to discard any. You can get all that you want out of your life, just that the order of things may not be the way you expect them to be. Have the right attitude and see your life change for the good. Your life is all yours; go for it, live it to the fullest! Set your attitude right and take the world in your stride!

Do not make yourself dependent on others' opinions to grow. Have confidence in yourself and do your best.

Think about the things that drive you high in life. What is the one thing you like to spend your time thinking about the most? Who or what fills you up with energy and uplifts your mood? When you find the answer, it will be the real driving force of your life that can change you for good and make you build your career. Focus on the ones that bring out the best in you.

During teenage, there can be many things that become either inspiration or distraction of life; for example, some incidents, friends, people you date, hobbies, books, actors, sports, and more. They all hold their good points and bad points and you must know-how. We shall discuss them soon in another book ;)

People you are close to, like your best friends, parents, teachers, and well-wishers, can also prove not worthy if YOU do not learn to remain humble and aim to be worth enough. Does it sound absurd?

Well, let us figure out how you mess up your life with things and people once you lack the discipline in you.

Let us take it up one by one. Parents are the highest source of love and inspiration undoubtedly. It is good to do things to make them happy such that you get the life of your choice; But trying wrong means to fetch marks and ONLY to please them will not add to your confidence and will not make you worthy. It is good to take care of their happiness but not at the cost of giving up your values, dignity, and peace. Put in your best efforts, and that is how you can bring them happiness and yourself confidence.

You, as a student, must have the zeal to score the best by putting in your best efforts. If you give in your 100% and then achieve 60 % will be your deserved marks, there can be nothing better. Similarly, if you by wrong means score 90%, this distinction will not be enough. You must know your potential and work without excuses. Believe me that parents are aware of the capabilities of their children. Then no one can stop the parents get disappointed in seeing you perform below your capacity level.

Set your aim correctly. Do not be centred towards your parents. Be disciplined, work hard, utilise your time and focus towards a brighter future. Running short of time can also hinder your best performance; keep that in mind Dude!

F.R.I.E.N.D.S.

Ah! The world changes into a happening place when we talk about friends. There can be nothing better than having a great set of friends. Belonging to a group and living with a company is a heavenly feeling. On the other hand, if you quit a group of friends out of circumstances, you might feel it as one of the worst things that could happen to you. F.R.I.E.N.D.S are needed, and life is rocking because they make the world a better place to live. I agree with it all, yet do not make the mistake of making them your focus. As much as you determine your priority on friends, such should be on your career; do not mix them up. Your likes and your feelings solely belong to you, and you have the authority over them. Do not give your lens of mind the wrong focus to click. It will tend to capture useless images. Work as time demands. Friends are indispensable, give them their due importance but not the entire focus of your life. Focus on a career with friends by your side.

Friends are of all kinds; they may be both real and fake. They will support you, some of them will become your guiding star, some might go out of their way to help you, some will talk behind your back, some might envy you, some will find better friends and forget you. Have you heard the Hindi song *"Har ek friend zaroori hota hai…"*? it is entirely relatable. Each and everyone you meet will give you a lesson for your life. It is upon you how much you can learn from them.

Focus

We all have different choices, interests, and mood swings. Everyone has the right to live the life of their choice, but do not compromise on your values and ethics for keeping the friendship alive with people who want you to sail in their boat. As we know that excess of anything is bad, refrain from dominating or intruding into anyone's life. Instead, grow and help your friends grow with you. Else, I'm afraid you might lose yourself or find yourself alone, or you might always be on the hunt for new friends.

While in school and college, you make friends who you feel would stay for a lifetime. You may even decide to stay together forever, but as per diversity of interests, you never know what the future has in store for you. Later, you may be astonished to see that you seldom meet each other due to many obvious reasons. You will also find friends for life, and they will always be by your side irrespective of the physical distance. Make as many friends as you can, but always learn to focus on your life and not on them. Being dependent on a friend or living a life based on friendship is not a stable foundation for life.

It is natural to crave materialistic possessions like the latest video game, mobile phone, high-end branded clothes, latest bags, trending shoes, fastest cars, hairstyle, and makeup. These things are good to possess and enjoy. Again, it is good to accomplish them and enjoy. Aim to earn them with hard work and sincerity instead.

The only thing that will matter is your confidence and attitude. Not the quality of your materials, but the quality of your inner self decides and tags you as to what kind of a person you are. It is called goodwill and reputation and will remain even after your life ends.

Failure

Let us talk about those who cannot accept failure, and your whole life revolves around school, college, exams, and career. Among the teens, many focus their life entirely on getting the best grades. They cannot accept getting lower than other mates and want to excel everywhere.

It is good to have a goal, and strive for it again, do not forget that your focus should be learning. Teens become obsessed with getting the best grades, and they lose their peace of mind for it. They might have fewer friends or no genuine friends because their focus remains only on obtaining the best and nothing more than that. Do not fall into the pit by running a rat race for success. One day you might regret being left with nothing to be happy. Your true purpose as a student is to learn and gain knowledge.

Your focus is a difficult thing to win over. Never underestimate yourself; you can do wonders once you master the art of focussing in the correct place and at the right time.

Dislike

Often you dislike a set of people, or maybe individuals, for who they are or how they are towards you. This attitude negatively affects your life altogether. You must understand that by disliking anyone, you are bringing your focus on them. You tend to build your feelings around the things they do. Do not rent out your mental space to them; it isn't worth it. It can so happen in the case of a friend you dislike, or a teacher, your ex-girlfriend/boyfriend, co-worker, and others. Isn't this an absolute waste of time? Why waste time on others by valuing their negativity.

Balance

The most important of all is to keep a balance in life. After discussing so many points, we clearly understand that focussing too much on self is not good either. Your life cannot just revolve around your worries. They will only pull you down, shift your thoughts towards building opportunities. Problems, when termed as challenges, can be dealt with well. Worrying about things leads to more trouble and can be hazardous.

You must have a passion for everything. You must also take care of the little things that make your parents happy; you must make friends and be social, you should be helpful, kind and generous, you must have the aim to become big, and remember life is not a bed of roses you will have to face problems.

Draw a fine line between people-pleasing and pursuing your dreams. Take up things rightly, stick to that line, and do not focus beyond it.

All you can do and must do is to define good rules and principles for yourself. Follow them and see your life change for good. You will be able to keep the balance in life and find yourself happy.

Aim to follow these principles with determination. You can rule the world once you make correct principles to follow. You will have a balanced focus once you religiously follow your decisions.

CHAPTER 21

THE TRICKY TEENS

HAPPY NOTE FROM TEENS

Tasks for Parents

Did you go through the multiple pages of tasks assigned for the teens in the previous chapter? It contains more than two thousand words. Phew! Such a long lecture, what else did you expect? Well, whoever said that Hitler is dead must meet my mom. Is that the case with your mom too? Just kidding, LOL.

Jokes apart, believe me, or not our parents are the kinds who care a lot about their relationship with us. They are searching for advice for connecting better with us. This may be one reason why you have this book with you, buddy!

We children do not always know how to let our parents know what we need. We try to protect them from the complexities of our life. Do you guys agree? For this reason and some more, we do not always choose to share all that we feel. Despite love and affection, their goal should not be to know everything about us but to be there when we need them.

NOTE TO PARENTS

Dear parents, *you are the kind of parent who cares so much as you seek strategies to help us meet our challenges. We do understand that there are no people more committed than parents in raising their children. You even have your own life examples and guide us with the wisdom of*

131

your experience. But we promise you that the best research, scientists, psychologists, counsellors, who are committed to teen development will not be able to help you more than us – your own kids. We can guide you to precisely what is going on with us and how we want you to be. Just hear us out without judging and by keeping your perspective away.

No books, not even this one, can guide you to what kind of environment we are looking for; no one can tell you about our peers and pressures. You do not know about our thoughts and feelings, and no one other than us can ever be your perfect guide.

Now you understand that you are lucky to have been living with your expert Teen kids.

What can parents learn from us – their teenage kids?

There are so many things teenagers would want their parents to learn. We want them to understand our perspective about certain things. Let me share the ones I could think of.

1. Bringing about small changes is a big deal for kids. Parents are so much settled in their way of lifestyle that it really takes a great deal to bring them out and make them feel comfortable with our lifestyle.

2. Parents get over-worried for several matters they can chill about, which leads to overreactions at times. For example, they would worry about their child not passing the exam because they did not give time to books as per their expectations. They must take life more optimistically.

3. Parents must be open to constructive criticism. They must give an ear to the change we want to see in them and not just write a book on it, mind you!

4. They must learn to relax about some matters that are usually tiny, but parents tag them huge issues. For example: We do understand that addiction of alcohol is bad, and we expect you to agree that trying alcohol in the appropriate age is fair. Their rigid restrictions uplift our cravings, addiction comes later.

5. They should be more understanding about the kind of clothes we want to wear for the outings. They find cool and trendy clothes skimpy and unfit to wear.

6. They must stop asking too many questions about our social matters that are irrelevant to them. We do not need to update who we had a fight with or the ongoing conflict within our social group!

7. They must understand that not every secret can be shared with them, and it no more remains a secret. Moreover, these secrets are childhood memories that we can talk about and laugh out about later.

8. They can excuse us on petty matters and not remain adamant about seeking an immediate apology on the same. We can discuss things after a break.

9. They should be considerate and a bit lenient about junk food; allow us to enjoy while we eat and store their lecture for later, please.

10. Demanding an A+ grade or a 95% from us is not fair at all. It can definitely add pressure on us leading to increased stress and lower performance level. Parents with disappointed eyes can actually dishearten their children and make them feel unworthy. Reminding us of our capabilities is necessary so that we put in our best efforts.

We, the tricky teens!

Now you can conclude that we (the teens) are easy and uncomplicated and not tricky at all. Talk to us before judging, assuming, blaming, restricting or demanding. We know the tricks and can teach you (parents and adults) how to deal with us. But you, our parents, are the magicians; you possess the magic wand to transform us; all you need to learn are the right tricks, and ...Abracadabra...Lo and behold...you now have a mutually understanding, open, happy, warm, respectful, affectionate, flexible, and ever-lasting relationship. We love you Mum and Dad! (hugs)

STRAIGHT FROM THE HEARTS OF MY CO-AUTHORS

"I feel teenage is all about having fun, making memories, and enjoying. Although it's different for everyone with ups and downs. Mostly it's figuring out about yourself and keeping yourself first. I want this phase to be a memorable part of my life so that once I look back at it, I feel happy. I think parents should not restrict kids from having fun of their choice. Teens' must be allowed to do things the way they want to and not be burdened with an opinion on everything. Parents should try to be supportive of their friends and studies. And make this already difficult time a little bit easier for us!"

-Tanvi Killa (co-author)

Class XI

La Martiniere for Girls School

"Hi, I am Avni Killa & I'm 12 and gonna turn into a teen very soon this year. But I already feel like one! I belong to a family where everything is allowed which even a 12yr old child wouldn't be allowed, I'm proved for that but I'm still waiting for few things which I feel should be allowed. Does it even happen with you all? I love dancing, and my parents encourage me and cheer me to become a great dancer. My mom allowed me to make an account on Insta, whereas I see people elder to me aren't allowed, I'm happy for it that she allowed. But my sis Tanvi di is allowed more things than me whether it is about phone, series or outing with friends. I want to have all the fun that she has without me. So teenage I'm coming to you."

-Avni Killa (Co-author)

Class VIII

La Martiniere for Girls School

SYNOPSIS BEE MAGICAL

Explore the unparalleled techniques of creating your life the way you want it to be. Special powers will take you on a miraculous journey of knowing your real purpose in this incarnation. Discover the tricks of survival in the enchanted garden and be benefitted!

The magic dust spreads more and more when you attempt to give back whatever you can. No matter how big or small, the happiness you receive by giving will be everlasting. The joy and satisfaction that come from helping another person make his life better are truly magical.

This wonderful journey ends with you questioning yourself about your own existence. The Universe, along with the guiding stars, healing angels and magic spells, unites to create a world that will never be the same. It's time to reveal the magnificent!